HAL LEONARD KEYBOARD STYLE SERIES

JAZZ-BLUES PIANO

THE COMPLETE GUIDE WITH AUDIO!

To access audio visit:
www.halleonard.com/mylibrary
Enter Code
5237-2306-5241-3250

BY MARK HARRISON

ISBN 978-0-634-06224-7

T0052932

HAL•LEONARD®
CORPORATION
7777 W. BLUEMOUND RD. P.O. BOX 13819 MILWAUKEE, WI 53213

In Australia Contact:
Hal Leonard Australia Pty. Ltd.
4 Lentara Court
Cheltenham, Victoria, 3192 Australia
Email: ausadmin@halleonard.com

Visit Hal Leonard Online at www.halleonard.com

INTRODUCTION

Welcome to *Jazz-Blues Piano*. If you're interested in applying blues techniques to your jazz piano playing but were never quite sure how, then you've come to the right place! Whatever your playing level, this book will help you sound more authentic in your jazz-blues stylings.

After reviewing some essential chords and scales, we'll dig into the voicing techniques and rhythmic patterns that are vital for the jazz-blues pianist. We'll focus on "comping" (accompaniment) styles, as well as playing melodies and solos. This will help you to impart that blues feeling to your jazz piano performance!

In the process, we'll also see how jazz-blues styles evolved by combining jazz harmonies and rhythms with blues melodies, phrasing, and song structures. We'll spotlight some of the important jazz-blues pianists of the twentieth century, and see how to incorporate their vocabulary into your own music.

Seven complete tunes in various jazz-blues styles are included in the "Style File" chapter at the end of the book. All of these examples include transcribed keyboard solos. Jam with the rhythm section on these tunes using the play-along audio–this is a great way to develop your keyboard chops within these different styles.

Good luck with your Jazz-Blues Piano!

—*Mark Harrison*

About the Audio

On the accompanying audio you'll find demonstrations of most of the music examples in the book. The solo piano tracks feature the left-hand piano part on the left channel, and the right-hand piano part on the right channel, for easy "hands separate" practice. The full band tracks feature the rhythm section on the left channel and the piano on the right channel, so that you can play along with the band. Also, the Chapter 6 examples (creating melodies and solos) each have an extra track with the right-hand piano part on the right channel, and the left-hand piano part and the rhythm section all on the left channel, in case you need to practice just the right-hand part along with the band. This is all designed to give you maximum flexibility when practicing! Please see the individual chapters for specific information on the audio tracks and how to use them.

About the Author

Mark Harrison is a *Keyboard Magazine* columnist and an educational author whose books are used by thousands of musicians worldwide. His TV credits include *Saturday Night Live*, *American Justice*, *Celebrity Profiles*, and many other shows and commercials. As a working keyboardist in the Los Angeles area, Mark performs regularly with the top-flight Steely Dan tribute band Doctor Wu, as well as the critically-acclaimed Mark Harrison Quintet. He has also shared the stage with top musicians such as John Molo (Bruce Hornsby band) and Jimmy Haslip (Yellowjackets), and is currently co-writing an R&B/pop project with the GRAMMY®-winning songwriter Ron Dunbar. For further information on Mark's musical activities and education products, please visit *www.harrisonmusic.com*.

CONTENTS

Chapter 1
WHAT IS JAZZ-BLUES?

Jazz and blues are both indigenous American music styles that emerged in the late 19th and early 20th centuries, and they both have similar roots in African-American culture. From this early period until the present day, the development paths of jazz and blues have been intertwined to varying degrees. The term "jazz-blues" is used to describe music which significantly combines jazz and blues elements. The jazz elements typically include the rhythms, more advanced harmonies (compared to basic blues) and more sophisticated improvisation (using different chord/scale relationships). The blues elements include the form or song structure, use of dominant chords built from different scale degrees, and the melodies based on blues scales.

This book mainly focuses on the jazz styles from the mid-20th century, and how they were influenced by the blues. From the swing band era of the 1930s, to the jazz-rock of the 1970s and beyond, we will see how the important pianists in these styles developed the unique hybrid known as "jazz-blues."

Swing/Big Band (1930s)

Famous big bands from this period would often perform tunes with a twelve-bar blues form, for example "Basie's Thought" (Count Basie) and "22 Cent Stomp" (Duke Ellington). These tunes often had sparse and/or repetitive melodies which owed a lot to the blues, and the improvisation would similarly be "bluesy" in nature. Jimmy Rushing also added a distinctive blues-based vocal style when working with the Count Basie band. Otherwise, the instrumentation and arrangements were rooted in the the jazz swing stylings of the period.

Jump Blues (1940s/50s)

Jump blues was created by fusing together jazz, blues, swing, and pop elements. This was essentially dancing and party music, featuring "honkers" (saxophone players) and "shouters" (vocalists). The style was noted for driving rhythms, and laid the groundwork for the R&B and rock 'n' roll styles to come. Noted jump blues pianists included Big Joe Turner, Amos Milburn, and Floyd Dixon.

Bop or Bebop (1940s)

The bebop era featured small combos (contrasting with the big band period), using more adventurous harmonies and improvisation. This was music for listening rather than dancing. Bop musicians would often perform blues tunes, but with more intricate melodies, and reharmonized versions of the standard blues chord progressions. Noted bop pianists include Thelonious Monk, Bud Powell, and Erroll Garner.

Hard Bop (1950s)

The hard bop period represented a bluesier, harder-edged development of bebop, often with simplified melodies and phrasing. The piano great Horace Silver was an innovator in the use of blues elements within the hard bop style. Other great hard bop composers and instrumentalists included John Coltrane and Miles Davis, who was a seminal figure across various jazz styles and eras.

Cool Jazz (1950s/60s)

The cool jazz period was a contrast to the edginess and intricacy of bebop, with a more restrained feel and tempered dynamics, and the use of slower tempos. The Miles Davis *Kind of Blue* album is among the most famous examples of this style. Blues melodies and form were used in numerous cool jazz tunes. Noted pianists from this period include Bill Evans, Wynton Kelly, and Lennie Tristano.

Soul Jazz (1950s/60s)

Soul jazz featured prominent blues and gospel influences, and was a simpler, more rhythmic development of hard bop. This was "feel good" music, with a danceable groove often emphasized with "backbeats" from the drummer. The piano and vocal stylings of Mose Allison are a good representation of this style. Other noted soul jazz pianists include Gene Harris, and the aforementioned Horace Silver, another innovator in multiple jazz styles/eras.

Jazz/Rock Fusion (late 1960s/70s)

The jazz/rock period combined rock rhythms and electronic instruments with jazz harmony and improvisation. Blues melodic concepts, phrasing, and form influenced many tunes from this period. Rhythms used were often "straight" rather than "swing" (eighth or sixteenth notes). This is another jazz style in which Miles Davis was a great innovator, and his *Bitches Brew* album is an all-time classic from this period. Noted pianists and keyboardists who emerged from this era include Herbie Hancock, Joe Zawinul, and Chick Corea.

Because jazz and blues are so intertwined, many famous pianists are adept across the range of jazz and blues styles and their combinations. This is one reason why drawing a rigid dividing line between jazz and blues is neither possible nor practical. As long as jazz and blues styles continue, they will continue to nourish one another, and create great music along the way!

Now we'll review the chords and scales needed to play jazz-blues (in Chapter 2), before focusing on keyboard voicings and comping patterns (starting in Chapter 3). On with the show!

SCALES and CHORDS

Major scales and modes

First of all, we'll take a look at the **major scale**, which is the fundamental basis of harmony in most contemporary music styles. I recommend that you think of this scale in terms of the intervals it contains—whole step, whole step, half step, whole step, whole step, whole step and half step—as this most closely parallels how the ear relates to the scale. Here is the C major scale, showing these intervals:

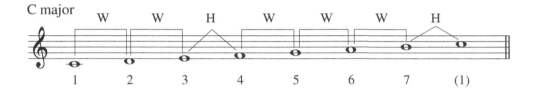

Here, for your reference, are all of the major scales. After the first scale (C major), the next seven scales contain flats, i.e., F major has one flat, B♭ major has 2 flats, and so on. The next seven scales contain sharps, i.e., G major has one sharp, D major has 2 sharps, and so on.

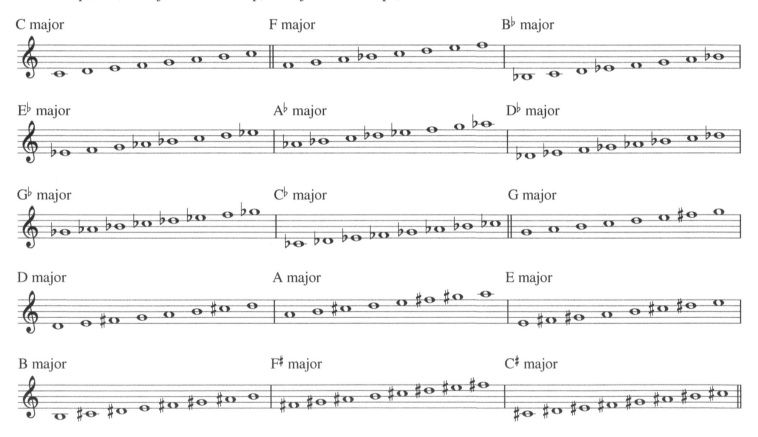

In this book, we'll work with music examples in different major and minor keys. For example, a tune will be "in the key of C major" if the note C is heard as the tonic or "home base," and if the notes used are within the C major scale (except for any raised or lowered notes occurring in the music). Similarly, a tune will be "in the key of A minor" if the note A is heard as the tonic or "home base," and if the notes used are within an A minor scale (again, except for any raised or lowered notes).

A **key signature** is a group of flats or sharps at the beginning of the music that lets you know which key you are in. Each key signature works for both a **major** and a **minor** key, which are considered relative to one another. For example, the first key signature shown below (no sharps and no flats) works for both the keys of C major and A minor. To find out which minor key shares the same key signature as a major key, we identify the 6th degree of the corresponding major scale, i.e. the 6th degree of a C major scale is the note A, so the keys of C major and A minor are relative to one another and share the same key signature.

Here for your reference are all of the major and minor key signatures:

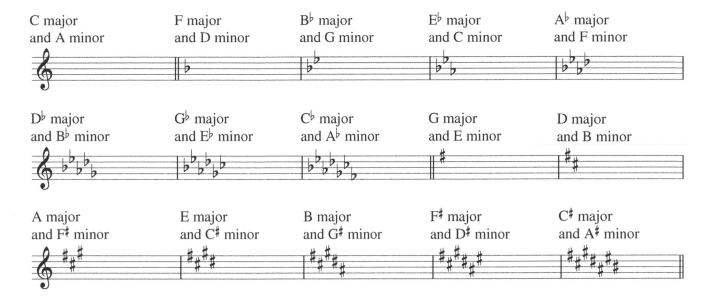

A **mode** or modal scale is created when we take a major scale and displace it to start on another scale degree. An example of this is the **Dorian** mode, created when the major scale is displaced to start on the 2nd degree, as in the following example of a C major scale displaced to create a D Dorian mode:

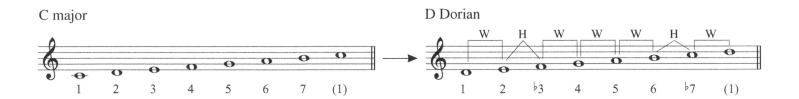

If you compare the two scales above, you'll see that the notes are the same; they just begin (and end) differently. Each has a different tonic or root, and a different pattern of whole and half steps. You can also think of the Dorian mode as a major scale with a lowered 3rd and 7th (1–2–♭3–4–5–6–♭7). This mode has a minor sound and is a basic scale source for a **minor 7th chord** (more about chords shortly). Another important mode in jazz-blues styles is the **Mixolydian** mode, which is the basic scale source for a **dominant 7th chord**, and is therefore very useful when creating parts over dominant harmonies. This mode is created when the major scale is displaced to start on the 5th degree:

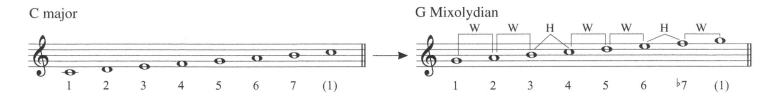

You can also think of the Mixolydian mode as a major scale with a lowered 7th (1–2–3–4–5–6–♭7).

Pentatonic and blues scales

The **major pentatonic** scale (a.k.a. the pentatonic scale) is a five-note scale often used in jazz-blues, as well as in R&B and pop styles. It can be derived by taking the major scale and removing the 4th and 7th degrees:

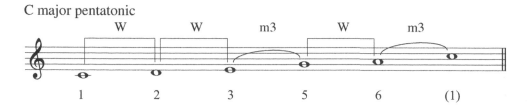

Note that from bottom to top, this scale contains the following intervals: whole step, whole step, minor 3rd, whole step, and minor 3rd.

The **minor pentatonic** scale (a.k.a. blues pentatonic) can be derived from the major pentatonic scale. For example, if we now take the C pentatonic scale and displace it to start on the note A (which is the relative minor of C), we create an A minor pentatonic scale, as follows:

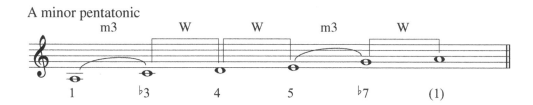

Note that from bottom to top, this scale now contains the following intervals: minor 3rd, whole step, whole step, minor 3rd, and whole step.

Finally, the **blues scale** can be derived by adding one note, the ♯4/♭5, to the minor pentatonic scale. For example, if we take the A minor pentatonic scale and add the "connecting tone" D♯ between the notes D and E, we create an A blues scale, as follows:

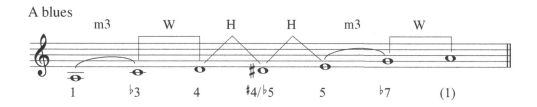

The blues scale is especially useful in jazz-blues applications, and you should make it a goal to learn this important scale in all keys, as follows:

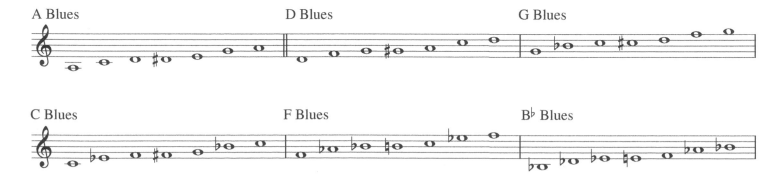

Natural and melodic minor scales

Next, we'll take a look at two of the **minor scales** which occur in jazz-blues styles. If we stay within a minor key without using any extra accidentals (sharps or flats) in the music, that means we are using a **natural minor** scale. Again, it is good to think of this scale in terms of the intervals it contains. Here is the C natural minor scale, showing these intervals:

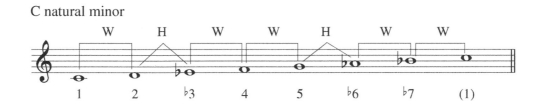

You can also think of the natural minor scale as a major scale with a lowered 3rd, 6th and 7th (1–2–♭3–4–5–♭6–♭7). Note that this scale is also equivalent to the 6th mode of a major scale (known as the **Aeolian** mode). If we were to take the E♭ major scale and displace it to start on the 6th degree (C), the above scale would be created.

Next, we will look at the melodic minor scale, which is often used when improvising over altered harmonies in more advanced jazz-blues styles. Here is the C melodic minor scale, again showing the internal intervals:

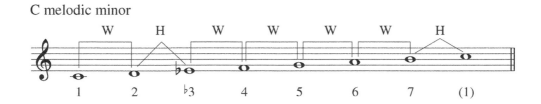

You can also think of the melodic minor scale as a major scale with a lowered 3rd (1–2–♭3–4–5–6–7). Classical or traditional theory often distinguishes between different ascending and descending forms of this scale; however, this distinction is not required for contemporary applications. Later, in Chapter 6, we will see how these minor scales are used when soloing in jazz-blues styles.

Triads

There are four main types of triad (three-part chord) in common usage: **major**, **minor**, **augmented**, and **diminished**. The following example shows all of these triads, built from the root of C in each case:

Note that these triads are formed by building the following intervals above the root note:

Major triad:	Major 3rd and perfect 5th (1–3–5)
Minor triad:	Minor 3rd and perfect 5th (1–♭3–5)
Augmented triad:	Major 3rd and augmented 5th (1–3–♯5)
Diminished triad:	Minor 3rd and diminished 5th (1–♭3–♭5)

If we construct triads from each degree of the major scale, and stay within the restrictions of the scale, we create **diatonic** triads. The following example shows the diatonic triads found within the C Major scale:

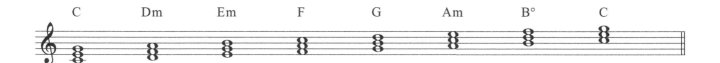

Relating the above triads to the four main triad types, note that major triads are built from the 1st, 4th and 5th major scale degrees, minor triads are built from the 2nd, 3rd, and 6th scale degrees, and a diminished triad is built from the 7th scale degree. (The augmented triad does not occur anywhere in the diatonic series).

Seventh (or four-part) chords and alterations

The term "seventh chord" is sometimes used to describe four-part chords in which the highest note or extension is the 7th above the root. The four-part chords most commonly used in jazz-blues are the **major 7th**, **minor 7th**, **dominant 7th**, **suspended dominant 7th**, and **diminished 7th** chords. The following example shows these four-part chords, built from the root of C:

Note that these chords are formed by building the following intervals above the root note:

Major 7th chord:	Major 3rd, perfect 5th, and major 7th intervals
Minor 7th chord:	Minor 3rd, perfect 5th, and minor 7th intervals
Dominant 7th chord:	Major 3rd, perfect 5th, and minor 7th intervals
Suspended Dominant 7th chord:	Perfect 4th, perfect 5th and minor 7th intervals
Diminished 7th chord:	Minor 3rd, diminished 5th and diminished 7th intervals

It is also possible to alter the major, minor and dominant 7th chords by lowering or raising the 5th of the chord by one half step. Of these possibilities, the following four-part chord alterations are the most useful in jazz-blues styles:

Each of these chords is an alteration of one of the previous four-part chords, as follows:

- the Cmaj7♭5 and Cmaj7♯5 chords can be derived by altering the 5th of the major 7th chord.

- the Cm7♭5 chord can be derived by lowering the 5th of the minor 7th chord.

- the C7♯5 chord can be derived by raising the 5th of the dominant 7th chord. Note that the chord symbol C+7 can also be used for this chord; the "+" symbol means that the 5th is raised.

These altered chords can also be formed by building the following intervals above the root note:

Major 7th (♭5) chord:	Major 3rd, diminished 5th and major 7th intervals
Major 7th (♯5) chord:	Major 3rd, augmented 5th and major 7th intervals
Minor 7th (♭5) chord:	Minor 3rd, diminished 5th and minor 7th intervals
Dominant 7th (♯5) chord:	Major 3rd, augmented 5th and minor 7th intervals

If we construct four-part chords from each degree of the major scale, and stay within the restrictions of the scale, we create diatonic four-part chords. The following example shows the diatonic four-part chords found within the C Major scale:

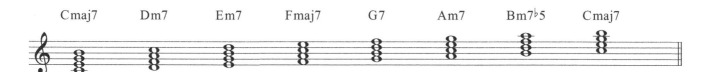

Relating the above four-part chords to those previously shown, note that major 7th chords are built from the 1st and 4th major scale degrees, minor 7th chords are built from the 2nd, 3rd, and 6th scale degrees, a dominant 7th chord is built from the 5th scale degree, and a minor 7th (♭5) chord is built from the 7th scale degree.

Ninth (or five-part) chords and alterations

The term "ninth chord" is sometimes used to describe five-part chords in which the highest note or extension is the 9th above the root. The five-part chords most commonly used in jazz-blues styles are the **major 9th**, **minor 9th**, **dominant 9th**, and **suspended dominant 9th**. The following example shows these four-part chords, built from the root of C:

Note that these five-part chords can all be formed by taking four-part chords previously shown (major 7th, minor 7th, dominant 7th, suspended dominant 7th) and adding a major 9th interval to each. We can analyze the intervals in each of these five-part chords as follows:

Major 9th chord:	Major 3rd, perfect 5th, major 7th and major 9th intervals
Minor 9th chord:	Minor 3rd, perfect 5th, minor 7th and major 9th intervals
Dominant 9th chord:	Major 3rd, perfect 5th, minor 7th and major 9th intervals
Suspended Dominant 9th chord:	Perfect 4th, perfect 5th, minor 7th and major 9th intervals

It is also possible to alter the ninth of the dominant 9th chord by lowering or raising it by one half step. (Altering 9ths is limited to dominant chords in conventional Western music styles—i.e., we would not normally alter 9ths on major and minor chords). This altered 9th might then be combined with an altered 5th. The following are the most common combinations of dominant chord alterations in jazz-blues styles:

Note that all of these chords contain major 3rd and minor 7th intervals from the root, which is the essential structure of a dominant chord. Again we can analyze the intervals in each of these chords as follows:

Dominant 7th (♭9) chord:	Major 3rd, perfect 5th, minor 7th and minor 9th intervals
Dominant 7th (♯9) chord:	Major 3rd, perfect 5th, minor 7th and augmented 9th intervals
Dominant 7th (♯5, ♭9) chord:	Major 3rd, augmented 5th, minor 7th and minor 9th intervals
Dominant 7th (♯5, ♯9) chord:	Major 3rd, augmented 5th, minor 7th and augmented 9th intervals

Sometimes, you may encounter the chord symbol suffix "7alt," as in the chord symbol C7alt. This technically means that all alterations of the 5th and 9th are available on the dominant chord. A good "default" response in many of these situations is to raise the 5th and the 9th, as in the above C7♯9♯5 chord. Also you should be aware that the raised 5th is equivalent to a lowered 13th, and the lowered 5th is equivalent to a raised 11th. These suffixes are often used interchangeably within dominant chord symbols.

⁓

In this chapter, I've tried to summarize the essential music theory and harmony that will help you play jazz-blues on the piano. If you would like further information on these topics, please check out my other music instruction books, *Contemporary Music Theory (Levels 1-3)* and *The Pop Piano Book*. (All of these books are published by Hal Leonard Corporation.)

Chapter 3

KEYBOARD HARMONY and VOICINGS

Voicing concepts

Although it is important that you know how to spell the chords described in Chapter 2, be aware that the larger the chords get (especially ninth chords and above), the less likely you are to "voice" them on the keyboard in simple stacks of 3rds. A keyboard **voicing** is a specific allocation of notes between the hands, chosen to **interpret** the chord symbol in question. In other words, knowing how to spell the chords is one thing, but knowing how to voice them on the keyboard is quite another.

In jazz-blues styles, we will often make use of **upper structure** and **polychord** voicings. Upper structures are three- or four-part interior chords which are in turn "built from" a chord tone (i.e., 3rd, 5th, 7th, etc.) of the overall chord needed. Many of the triads and four-part chords we reviewed in the last chapter also function as upper structures on larger chords. This is a very efficient voicing method, not least because the same upper structures can be used within various different overall chords. Upper structures can then be played in the right hand (over the root or "root-7th" of the overall chord in the left hand), or in the left hand (below a melody or solo being played by the right hand).

In more modern jazz and jazz-blues settings, we can also play an upper structure in each hand, creating a polychord (meaning "chord-over-chord") voicing. In a jazz band or trio situation, the bass player would typically play the root of the chord below these "rootless" piano voicing combinations. Much more about these upper structure and polychord voicings shortly!

Major and minor triad inversions

As we will shortly see, the major triad is a very commonly used upper structure on different overall chords. Here are the inversions of a C major triad:

TRACK 1

Note that in the above example, the first triad shown is in **root position** (with the root on the bottom), the second triad is in **first inversion** (with the 3rd on the bottom), and the third triad is in **second inversion** (with the 5th on the bottom). The last triad is in root position, an octave higher than the first. To connect smoothly between successive voicings, it is important to have these inversions under your fingers in all keys. You should make it a goal to learn all the major triad inversions, as follows:

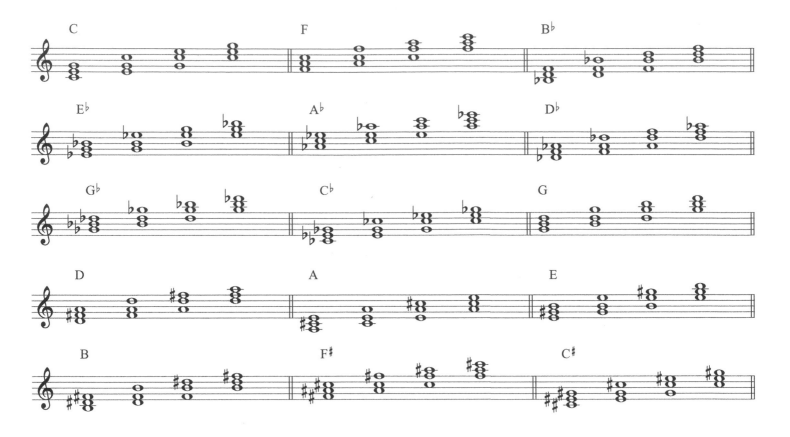

The minor triad is also very useful as an upper structure voicing. Here are the inversions of a C minor triad:

TRACK 2

The above example contains C minor triads in root position, first inversion, second inversion, and then root position again (similar to the previous major triad examples).

Learn these inversions in all keys, as shown in the following example:

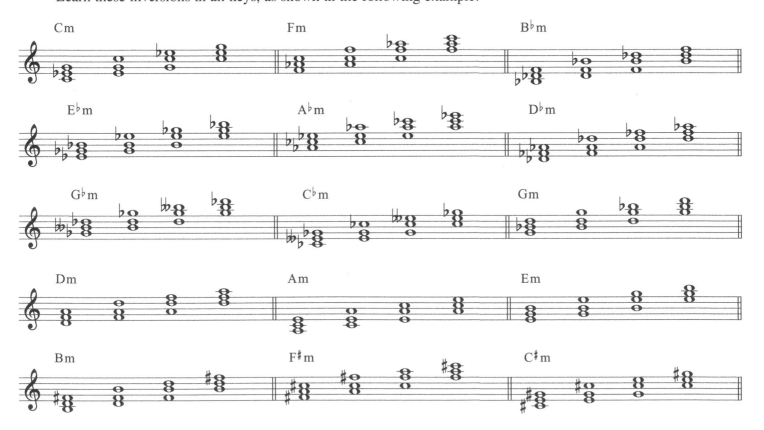

Triad-over-root chord voicings

The first upper structure technique we will present is the "triad-over-root" voicing. Different rules will apply depending upon what overall type of chord (i.e., major, minor, dominant etc.) we are trying to create. First we will look at the commonly used triad-over-root voicings for major and minor chords:

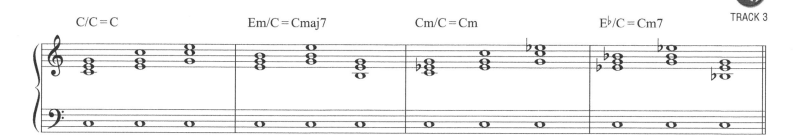

TRACK 3

We can make the following observations about this example, which will apply to all the upper structure voicings shown in this chapter:

- The upper structures in the right hand (triads in this case) are each "built from" different chord tones of the overall chord (from the root and 3rd of the C major chord, and the root and 3rd of the C minor chord, in this case). Each inversion of the upper structure is shown in the right hand. The root of the overall chord is played by the left hand each time.

- There are two chord symbols above each measure. The first is a "slash chord" symbol, with the upper structure on the left of the slash, and the root note on the right. The second is the equivalent "composite" symbol, showing the overall chord created by placing the upper structure over the root.

- Although both "slash" and "composite" are valid chord symbol styles, you are generally more likely to see composite symbols in a chart or fakebook. In order to use this upper structure voicing technique, you will therefore need to be able to derive a slash chord from a composite chord symbol. There are normally two ways in which this is done:

  - **Literal translation**: using an upper structure voicing, which when placed over the root, is exactly equivalent to the composite symbol. For example, if you see the chord symbol Cmaj7 and you respond with the second voicing shown (Em/C), you have exactly created a Cmaj7 chord between the hands, with no additional notes.

  - **Upgrading**: using an upper structure voicing, which when placed over the root, adds more notes/extensions to the composite symbol. For example, if you see the chord symbol Cm and you respond with the fourth voicing shown (E♭/C), you have added the 7th of the chord. Upgrading minor chord symbols this way is common across a range of jazz, blues, and pop styles.

Now we will analyze these specific major and minor chord voicings as follows:

- In the first measure, we are building a major triad from the root of the overall major chord (C/C). This is a simple triad-over-root voicing, and creates a basic major chord.

- In the second measure, we are building a minor triad from the 3rd of the overall major chord (Em/C). This creates a major seventh chord overall.

- In the third measure, we are building a minor triad from the root of the overall minor chord (Cm/C). This is a simple triad-over-root voicing, and creates a basic minor chord.

- In the fourth measure, we are building a major triad from the 3rd of the overall minor chord (E♭/C). This creates a minor seventh chord overall. (Note that E♭ is a minor third interval above the root of C).

Play each of the above voicings to get the sounds in your ears, and the shapes under your fingers!

Next we will look at triad-over-root voicings for altered minor, dominant, and suspended dominant chords:

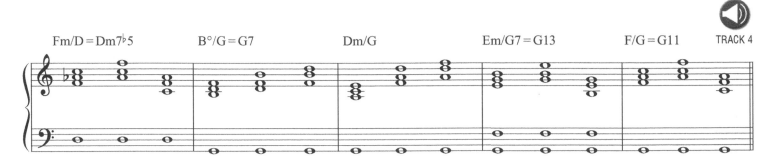

We can analyze these chord voicings as follows:

- In the first measure, we are building a minor triad from the 3rd of the overall minor chord (Fm/D). This creates a minor seventh chord, with a lowered 5th overall. (Note that F is a minor third above the root of D).

- In the second measure, we are building a diminished triad from the 3rd of the overall dominant chord (B°/G). This creates a dominant seventh chord overall.

- In the third measure, we are building a minor triad from the 5th of the overall chord (Dm/G). This creates a non-definitive sound which could be used on a minor, dominant, or suspended dominant chord (as no 3rd or 11th is present), which is why no composite chord symbol equivalent is shown. However, this combination is found within a G Mixolydian mode, and in jazz-blues it is often used with other "Mixolydian triads" to create or imply dominant harmonies—much more about Mixolydian triads later on!

- In the fourth measure, we are building a minor triad from the 13th (same as the 6th) of the overall dominant chord (Em/G7), with the left hand playing the 7th below. This creates a dominant 13th chord (in this case by adding the 13th to the dominant 7th) overall.

- In the fifth measure, we are building a major triad from the 7th of the overall suspended dominant chord (F/G). This creates a suspended dominant ninth (a.k.a. dominant eleventh) chord. (Note that F is a minor seventh interval above the root of G). The term "suspended" means that the 3rd of the dominant chord (B) has been replaced by the 4th/11th (C). This voicing can also work as a less defined or "incomplete" minor 11th chord.

Again, there are voicing upgrade possibilities here. For example, it is common practice in jazz and jazz-blues styles to upgrade basic dominant chord symbols by building the minor triad from the 13th, creating a dominant 13th chord overall. Now we'll see how to move between chords using these voicings and inversions. This progression has been voiced using the triad-over-root method:

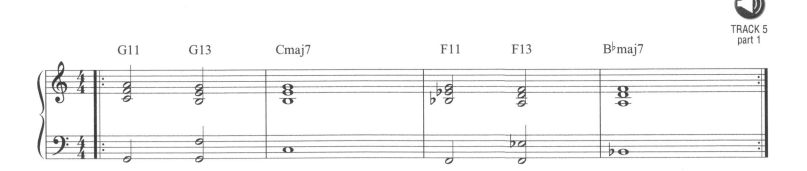

The G11 and G13 chords function as V chords (in other words, are built from the fifth scale degree) in the key of C. The Cmaj7 chord functions as a I (or "tonic" chord) in the key of C. Similarly, the F11 and F13 chords function as V chords in the key of B♭, and the B♭maj7 chord functions as a I (or "tonic" chord) in the key of B♭. The progression therefore consists of two V–I pairs, in the "momentary" (temporary) keys of C and B♭. Moving through different "momentary" keys in this way is routine in mainstream jazz styles, and is also found in more sophisticated jazz-blues tunes.

(For much more information on chord functions and momentary keys used in progressions, check out my *Contemporary Music Theory Level Two* book, also published by Hal Leonard Corporation.)

Note that we no longer have the triad-over-root (or "slash") chord symbols above the staff, in the preceding example— just the composite symbols (a realistic situation as is often seen in a chart or fake book). We need to look at each of these symbols and derive a triad-over-root voicing for each one. Then we need to voice lead smoothly between these upper structure triads, using inversions to avoid unnecessary interval skips. We can summarize the voicing choices as follows:

- In the first measure (beat 1), the G11 chord is voiced by building a major triad from the 7th (F/G).

- In the first measure (beat 3), the G13 chord is voiced by building a minor triad from the 13th (Em/G), with the left hand adding the 7th of the chord below.

- In the second measure, the Cmaj7 chord is voiced by building a minor triad from the 3rd (Em/C).

- In the third measure (beat 1), the F11 chord is voiced by building a major triad from the 7th (E♭/F).

- In the third measure (beat 3), the F13 chord is voiced by building a minor triad from the 13th (Dm/F), with the left hand adding the 7th of the chord below.

- In the fourth measure, the B♭maj7 chord is voiced by building a minor triad from the 3rd (Dm/B♭).

In the preceding example, all the upper structure triads are in second inversion, resulting in smooth voice leading through the progression. Now we will apply a simple eighth-note rhythm pattern to these voicings:

TRACK 5
part 2

Note that the audio track for this example was recorded using a "swing eighths" or "shuffle" feel, with the first eighth-note in each beat taking up two-thirds of the beat, and the next eighth-note taking up the remaining one-third of the beat (in other words, each pair of eighth notes sounds like a quarter note-eighth note triplet). This is the most common rhythmic feel used in jazz and jazz-blues styles. More about different rhythmic feels and subdivisions in Chapter 5!

Next, we'll create voicings for another progression, this time using two different II–V chord sequences:

TRACK 6
part 1

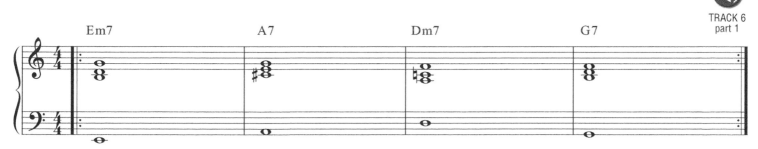

The Em7 and A7 chords function as a II and a V (in other words, are built from the second and fifth scale degrees) in the key of D, and similarly the Dm7 and G7 chords function as a II and a V in the key of C.

We can summarize the voicing choices in the preceding example as follows:

*   In the first measure, the Em7 chord is voiced by building a major triad from the 3rd (G/E).
*   In the second measure, the A7 chord is voiced by building a diminished triad from the 3rd (C#°/A).
*   In the third measure, the Dm7 chord is voiced by building a major triad from the 3rd (F/D).
*   In the fourth measure, the G7 chord is voiced by building a diminished triad from the 3rd (B°/G).

We can again apply a jazz-blues rhythmic pattern to these voicings, as follows:

TRACK 6
part 2

Again, this recording exhibits a swing-eighths feel, and uses typical eighth-note anticipations or **syncopations** (i.e., landing an eighth-note ahead of beat 1, before measures 2 and 4). These are very common rhythmic figures in jazz-blues, and across the range of mainstream jazz styles in general.

Next, we'll look at some triad-over-root voicings for altered dominant chords (where the 5th and/or 9th of the chord has been raised or lowered by a half step):

TRACK 7

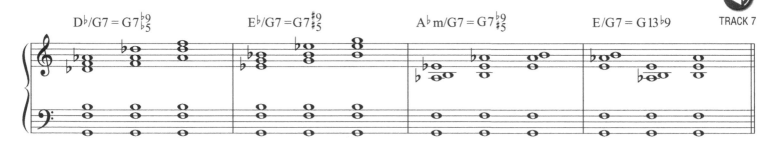

Note that in the left hand the 7th of the dominant chord (F) has been added, and in the first two measures the 3rd (B) has also been added. The 7th and 3rd are the definitive tones on the dominant (more about "7–3" voicings later on), and they are typically voiced below the altered 5ths and/or 9ths in mainstream jazz and jazz-blues styles. Don't worry if you can't stretch the root-7th-3rd voicing in the left hand—you can try omitting the 3rd (B) or the root (G). Also, depending on the upper triad inversion, the 3rd can be added using the thumb of the right hand, with the upper structure triad being played with the remaining fingers (as in measures 2 and 4 of Track 8, part 1).

We can analyze the upper triad voicings in the above example as follows:

*   In the first measure, we are building a major triad from the lowered 5th (equivalent to the raised 11th) of the overall dominant chord (Db/G7). Together with the 7th and 3rd added in the left hand, this creates a dominant seventh with lowered 5th and lowered 9th chord overall.

*   In the second measure, we are building a major triad from the raised 5th (equivalent to the lowered 13th) of the overall dominant chord (Eb/G7). Together with the 7th and 3rd added in the left hand, this creates a dominant seventh with raised 5th and raised 9th chord overall.

*   In the third measure, we are building a minor triad from the lowered 9th of the overall dominant chord (Abm/G7). Together with the 7th added in the left hand, this creates a dominant seventh with raised 5th and lowered 9th chord overall.

- In the fourth measure, we are building a major triad from the 13th of the overall dominant chord (E/G7). Together with the 7th added in the left hand, this creates a dominant thirteenth with lowered 9th chord overall.

(For much more information on dominant chord alterations, voicings, and scale source implications, check out my *Contemporary Music Theory Level Three* book, also published by Hal Leonard Corporation.)

Next, we'll use some of these voicings in a chord progression, as follows:

TRACK 8
part 1

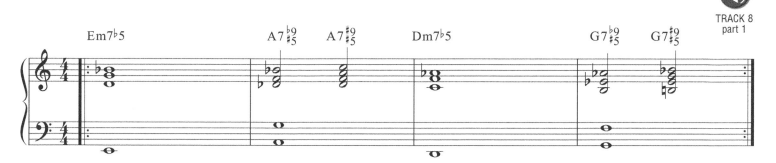

In jazz chord progressions, the altered minor 7th chord (i.e. the Em7♭5 in the first measure) will often function as a II chord in a minor key, and the altered dominant 7th chords (i.e., the A7♯5♭9 and A7♯5♯9 in the second measure) will often function as a V chord in a minor key. The above chord progression could therefore be thought of as a II–V in D minor, followed by a II–V in C minor.

We can summarize the voicing choices in the above example as follows:

- In the first measure, the Em7♭5 chord is voiced by building a minor triad from the 3rd (Gm/E).

- In the second measure (beat 1), the A7♯5♭9 chord is voiced by building a minor triad from the lowered 9th (B♭m/A7), with the 7th added in the left hand.

- In the second measure (beat 3), the right hand is playing four notes of the A7♯5♯9 chord. This can be thought of as an upper structure triad (top three notes), plus the 3rd of the chord being added (bottom note), played by the thumb—see comments following Track 7. The top three notes are a major triad built from the raised 5th (F/A7). The 7th is added in the left hand.

  (This can also be thought of as a four-part upper structure built from the 3rd of the dominant chord—more about this shortly).

- In the third measure, the Dm7♭5 chord is voiced by building a minor triad from the 3rd (Fm/D).

- In the fourth measure (beat 1), the G7♯5♭9 chord is voiced by building a minor triad from the lowered 9th (A♭m/G7), with the 7th added in the left hand.

- In the fourth measure (beat 3), the right hand is playing four notes of the G7♯5♯9 chord. This can be thought of as an upper structure triad (top three notes), plus the 3rd of the chord being added (bottom note). The top three notes are a major triad built from the raised 5th (E♭/G7). The 7th is again added in the left hand.

Next, we'll apply another jazz-blues rhythmic pattern to these voicings, as follows:

TRACK 8
part 2

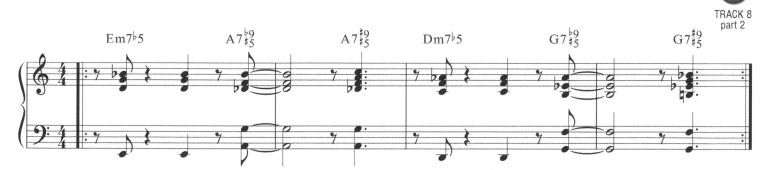

Mixolydian third intervals and patterns

Now we'll look at the use of 3rd intervals within Mixolydian modes, a common technique across the range of blues and jazz-blues styles. As the Mixolydian mode is a basic scale source for a dominant 7th chord, these patterns are well suited to the dominant chord progressions often found in jazz-blues. Grace notes which are a half step below the 3rd and/or 5th of the dominant chord can then be added for a "bluesier" effect. This example shows the C Mixolydian mode, together with the 3rds available within the mode:

TRACK 9
part 1

We can use the 3rd intervals in the right-hand measure above, to create patterns which will work on a C7 dominant chord, as follows:

TRACK 9
part 2

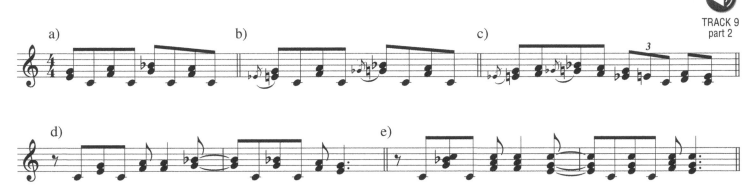

- Pattern a) uses the third intervals with the top notes consisting of the 5th, 13th (6th) and 7th of the implied C7 chord, alternating with the root (C) on all the upbeats.

- Pattern b) adds the grace notes E♭ before the E (♭3–3) and G♭ before the G (♭5–5).

- Pattern c) is a variation of b), using an eighth-note triplet figure during beat 3.

- Pattern d) is a two-measure phrase, using eighth-note anticipations/syncopations.

- Pattern e) is a variation of d), using a drone (repeated top note) of C above the third intervals.

Mixolydian triads and patterns

Next we will explore the use of Mixolydian triads to create patterns over dominant chords. If we take all the triads available within the C Mixolydian mode (which are the same as the diatonic triads in F Major, as C Mixolydian is a displaced version of an F major scale), invert them in either first or second inversion, and then place them over the bass note C, we get the following:

TRACK 10
part 1

C Mixolydian triads in first inversion   C Mixolydian triads in second inversion

E /C   F/C   Gm/C Am/C B♭/C   C   Dm/C E /C   E /C   F/C   Gm/C Am/C B♭/C   C   Dm/C E /C

Note the "slash" chord symbols, which describe each specific combination of upper triad over the bass note of C. Although these are correct chord symbols that we will sometimes see, it is better to think of these combinations as *all being available when interpreting a dominant 7th chord* (in this case a C7), i.e., we can improvise patterns by moving between these upper triads.

The first triad shown in both 1st and 2nd inversion (i.e., E°/C) together with the root note of C creates a C7 chord, as the notes in the E diminished triad (E, G and B♭) are the 3rd, 5th and 7th of the chord respectively. Because the E diminished triad (over the root of C) sounds the most stable with respect to the overall C7 chord, we will often start and/or end a Mixolydian triad right-hand phrase with this upper diminished triad. The other triads shown above contain various combinations of basic chord tones and upper extensions or **passing tones** of the overall dominant chord. These sound more unstable, and keep the music in motion. Now we'll use these upper triads in some comping patterns, as follows:

TRACK 10
part 2

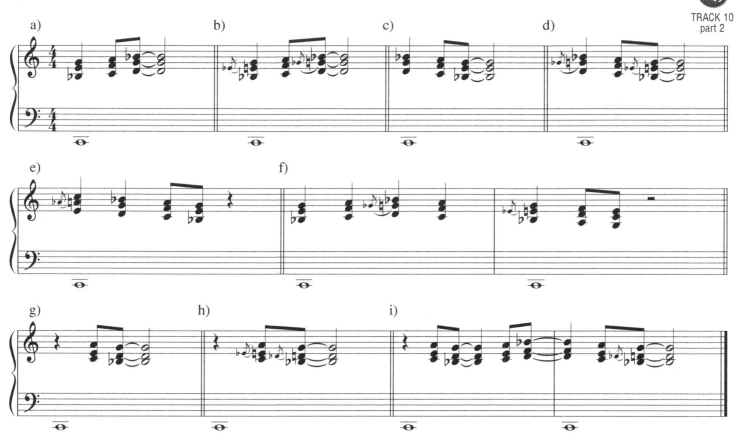

- Patterns a) – f) use 2nd inversion Mixolydian triads, and patterns g) – i) use 1st inversion Mixolydian triads.

- Pattern a) uses the triads with the top notes consisting of the 5th, 13th (6th), and 7th of the implied C7 chord, with the final G minor triad anticipating beat 3 by an eighth note.

- Pattern b) adds the grace notes E♭ before the E (♭3–3) and G♭ before the G (♭5–5).

- Pattern c) is a variation of a), using the upper triads in reverse order.

- Pattern d) is a variation of b), using the upper triads in reverse order.

- Pattern e) starts with the root (C) as the top note, and then descends through the 7th, 13th (6th) and 5th.

- Pattern f) is a two-measure phrase, with a mixture of upper triads and grace notes.

- Pattern g) moves between the two "adjacent" minor triads in the Mixolydian mode (in this case Am to Gm, both over C), creating a characteristic blues and jazz-blues figure.

- Pattern h) adds the grace notes E♭ before the D (♭3–3) and D♭ before the D (♭9–9).

- Pattern i) is a two-measure phrase, adding the B♭ triad to the previous two minor triads (Gm and Am).

Dorian triads and patterns

Now we will see how to use Dorian triads to create patterns over minor or minor 7th chords. If we take all the triads available within the D Dorian mode (which are the same as the diatonic triads in C Major—D Dorian is a displaced version of a C major scale), and then place them over the root of C, we get the following:

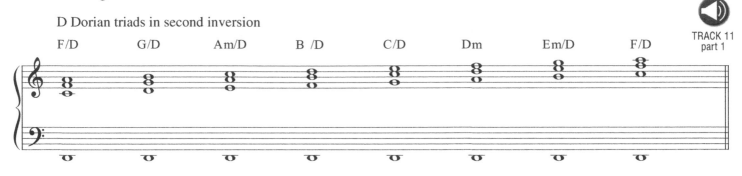

Here, we have just shown the upper triads in second inversion, although other inversions are of course available. Now we'll see these triads used in some rhythmic patterns, as follows:

These patterns use a sixteenth-note subdivision often found in the jazz-rock and R&B styles from the 1970s, onward (more about this later).

- Pattern a) moves between the two "adjacent" major triads in the Dorian mode (in this case, F to G, over D). This is a common Dorian harmonic figure across a range of jazz, blues and funk styles.

- Pattern b) adds the A minor triad into the mix, with the top notes moving between the 5th, 13th (6th), and 7th of the implied Dm7 chord. The grace note A♭, before the A (♭5–5) is also used.

- Pattern c) is a two-measure phrase, adding the two minor triads Em and Dm to those previously used.

22

Four-part chord inversions

The major 7th four-part chord is another useful upper structure on some larger chords. Here are the inversions of a C major seventh chord:

Note that in the above example, the first chord shown is in root position (with the root on the bottom), the second chord is in first inversion (with the 3rd on the bottom), the third chord is in second inversion (with the 5th on the bottom), and the fourth chord is in third inversion (with the 7th on the bottom). The first inversion major seventh chord sounds more dissonant due to the "exposed" half-step interval on top. Therefore, use care when employing this inversion. You should make it a goal to learn all the major seventh chord inversions, as follows:

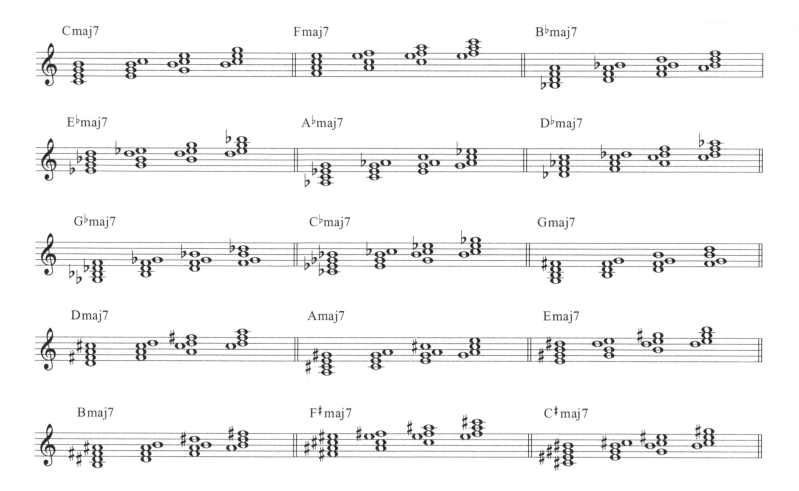

The minor 7th four-part chord, like the major 7th, is also a useful upper structure on larger chords. The following are the inversions of a C minor seventh chord:

The above example contains C minor 7th chords in root position, first inversion, second inversion, and third inversion (similar to the previous major 7th chord examples).

Again, you should learn these inversions in all keys, as shown in the following example:

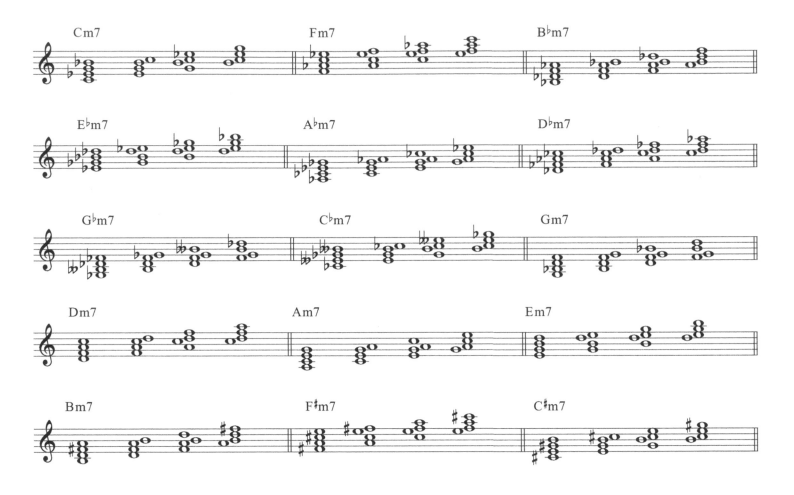

In Chapter 2 we saw that a minor 7th chord can be altered to a minor 7th ($\flat$5) chord, by lowering the 5th. The minor 7th ($\flat$5) chord is a useful upper structure when voicing dominant and altered harmonies in jazz-blues. Here are the first three m7$\flat$5 chords and inversions around the circle of 5ths. It is recommended that you become familiar with these in all keys:

TRACK 14

The dominant 7th chord is also a useful four-part chord shape for voicing dominant chords in more basic jazz-blues styles (although it is less useful as an upper structure on other chords). The following are the first three dominant 7th chords and inversions around the circle of 5ths. It is again recommended that you become familiar with these in all keys:

TRACK 15

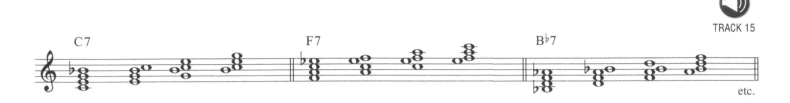

Four-part-over-root chord voicings

The next upper structure technique we will look at is the "four-part-over-root" voicing. This involves building a four-part interior chord from a chord tone (i.e., 3rd, 5th, 7th etc.) of the overall chord. Again, different rules will apply depending on what type of chord (i.e., major, minor, dominant etc.) we are trying to create. First we will look at the commonly used four-part-over-root voicings for major and minor chords:

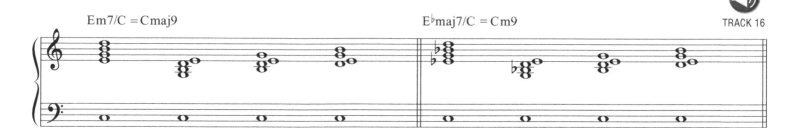

TRACK 16

Note that (as for the triad-over-root voicings) both slash chord and composite chord symbols are shown, and all inversions of the upper structures are shown. Again, the goal is to be able to interpret the composite symbol with a suitable upper structure voicing. We can analyze the above voicings as follows:

- In the first measure, we are building a minor 7th four-part chord from the 3rd of the overall major chord (Em7/C). This creates a major ninth chord overall.

- In the second measure, we are building a major 7th four-part chord from the 3rd of the overall minor chord (E♭maj7/C). This creates a minor ninth chord overall. (Note that E♭ is a minor third above the root of C).

Again, it is fairly common practice in jazz and jazz-blues styles (as well as in pop/R&B) to upgrade major 7th chord symbols by using the first voicing above, and to upgrade minor 7th chord symbols by using the second voicing above. In both cases the result is the addition of the 9th to the chord.

Next, we will look at a series of four-part-over-root voicings for dominant and suspended dominant chords:

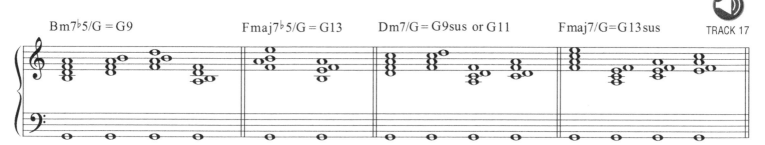

TRACK 17

The first two measures above contain voicings for **unsuspended** (or regular) dominant chords, which all contain the 3rd and 7th of the overall chord (B and F). The last two measures contain voicings for **suspended** dominant chords, in which the 3rd (B) has been replaced by the 4th/11th (C). These suspended voicings still contain the 7th of the chord (F). The above voicings are further analyzed as follows:

- In the first measure, we are building a minor 7th (♭5) four-part chord (Bm7♭5) from the 3rd of the overall dominant chord (G). This creates a dominant ninth chord overall.

- In the second measure, we are building a major 7th (♭5) four-part chord (Fmaj7♭5) from the 7th of the overall dominant chord (G). This creates a dominant thirteenth chord overall.

- In the third measure, we are building a minor 7th four-part chord (Dm7) from the 5th of the overall suspended dominant chord (G). This creates a suspended dominant ninth (or dominant eleventh) chord overall.

- In the fourth measure, we are building a major 7th four-part chord (Fmaj7) from the 7th of the overall suspended dominant chord (G). This creates a suspended dominant thirteenth chord overall.

When building upper structures from the 7th of the chord in measures 2 and 4 in the previous example, don't forget that F is a minor seventh interval above the root of G. Also note that in the second measure, the Fmaj7♭5 upper structure is only shown in root position and second inversion, as these are the most useful for this particular voicing. Next, we have some four-part-over-root voicings for altered dominant chords:

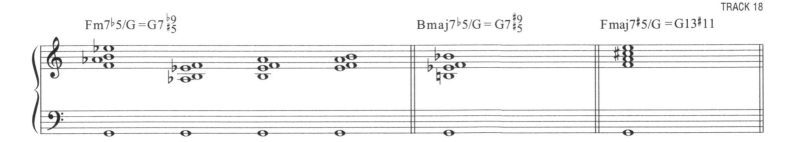

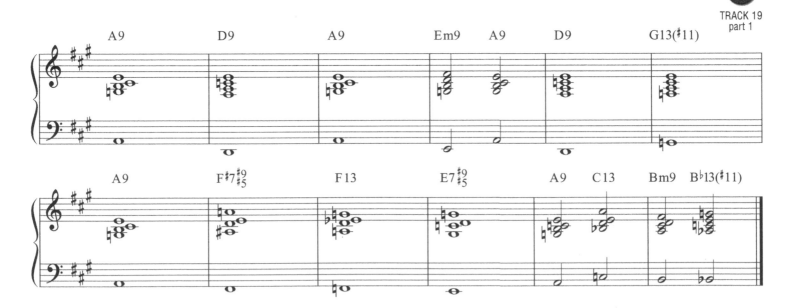

When notating these voicings, decisions are sometimes needed between different enharmonic alternatives (i.e., A♯ or B♭) for the same note. I recommend notating in a manner consistent with the key or scale being used. The above altered G7 voicings will most often function as V ("five") chords in the key of C minor, so, for example, the top note in the second measure (the raised 9th on the G7) has been notated as B♭ rather than A♯ for consistency with the implied key. These voicings are further analyzed as follows:

- In the first measure, we are building a minor 7th (♭5) four-part chord (Fm7♭5) from the 7th of the overall dominant chord (G). This creates a dominant seventh with raised 5th and lowered 9th chord overall.

- In the second measure, we are building a major 7th (♭5) four-part chord (Bmaj7♭5) from the 3rd of the overall dominant chord (G). This creates a dominant seventh with raised 5th and raised 9th chord overall.

- In the third measure, we are building a major 7th (♯5) four-part chord (Fmaj7♯5) from the 7th of the overall dominant chord (G). This creates a dominant thirteenth with raised 11th chord overall. (We saw earlier that a raised 11th is equivalent to a lowered 5th on the chord).

As in the previous dominant voicings, when building upper structures from the 7th of the chord, note that F is a minor seventh above the root of G. Also, some upper structures are shown just in root position, as this often works best on these more "altered" dominant chords.

Now we'll see how to move between chords using these four-part-over-root voicings and inversions. Starting with a 12-bar jazz-blues progression in the key of A, we will use some typical II–V and substitution chords (much more about different jazz-blues chord progressions in Chapter 4):

Again, we are only showing the composite chord symbols, and our job is to interpret these with suitable upper structure voicings. As with the previous triad-over-root progressions, once we have selected the four-part upper structures, we then need to invert them to ensure smooth voice leading. We can summarize the voicing choices as follows:

- In measures 1, 3, 4, 7 and 11, the A9 chord is voiced by building a minor 7th($\flat$5) four-part chord (C#m7$\flat$5) from the 3rd.

- In measures 2 and 5, the D9 chord is voiced by building a minor 7th($\flat$5) four-part chord (F#m7$\flat$5) from the 3rd.

- In measure 4 (beat 1), the Em9 chord is voiced by building a major 7th four-part chord (Gmaj7) from the 3rd.

- In measure 6, the G13#11 chord is voiced by building a major 7th(#5) four-part chord (Fmaj7#5) from the 7th.

- In measure 8, the F#7#5#9 chord is voiced by building a major 7th($\flat$5) four-part chord (A#maj7$\flat$5 or B$\flat$maj7$\flat$5) from the 3rd.

- In measure 9, the F13 chord is voiced by building a major 7th($\flat$5) four-part chord (E$\flat$maj7$\flat$5) from the 7th. Note this upper shape is used in second inversion.

- In measure 10, the E7#5#9 chord is voiced by building a major 7th($\flat$5) four-part chord (G#maj7$\flat$5, or A$\flat$maj7$\flat$5) from the 3rd.

- In measure 11 (beat 3), the C13 chord is voiced by building a major 7th($\flat$5) four-part chord (B$\flat$maj7$\flat$5) from the 7th.

- In measure 12 (beat 1), the Bm9 chord is voiced by building a minor 7th four-part chord (Dmaj7) from the 3rd.

- In measure 12 (beat 3), the B$\flat$13#11 chord is voiced by building a major 7th(#5) four-part chord (A$\flat$maj7#5) from the 7th.

Now we can apply a jazz-blues rhythmic pattern to these voicings:

TRACK 19
part 2

Notice the eighth-note anticipations (landing an eighth-note ahead of beats 1 and/or 3), emphasized by using the same rhythms in both hands. These are common features in jazz-blues styles and in mainstream jazz styles generally. These four-part upper structure voicings can also be used in the left hand, below a melody or solo part in the right hand. For this to work, the left-hand voicings generally need to be around the middle C area. This often means that the left hand will not be playing the root of the overall chord, which is why the term "rootless voicing" is sometimes used. If you are playing with a rhythm section, the root of the chord would typically be provided by the bass player. However, these voicings can also work for the solo pianist, as jazz and jazz-blues styles do not always require the root of the chord to be played (as opposed to most contemporary pop styles for example).

The next example shows a jazz-blues melody in the right hand, over the previous four-part voicings (now used in the left hand). There are two audio tracks for this example—one with piano only, and the other with a jazz-blues rhythm section with which to play along:

TRACK 20
piano only

TRACK 21
piano plus
rhythm section

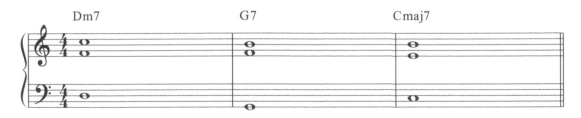

The left-hand rhythms are the same as used in the track 19, part 2 example. The right-hand melody part is derived from the A blues and F# blues scales (these are built from the tonic, and relative minor, of the key respectively). Much more about jazz-blues melody, phrasing and scale sources included in Chapter 6!

Seven-three chord voicings

The seven-three voicing is a staple jazz piano technique which is also useful in jazz-blues styles. It involves playing the seventh and third of the chord, which are the definitive "color" tones of any four-part chord, as in the following II–V–I progression example:

TRACK 22

Next we will make use of these seven-three voicings on a 12-bar jazz-blues progression in G:

All the chords in the above example have been voiced with the seven-three technique, and then voice leading is used to avoid unnecessary interval skips in the right hand. Jazz-blues rhythmic patterns can then be applied to the above voicings, as shown in the following example:

29

The previous example uses typical jazz syncopations, for example, the anticipations of beat 3 (in measure 1) and beat 2 (in measure 2), etc. Next we will combine a jazz-blues melody in the right hand, with these seven-three voicings (now played by the left hand). As the seven-three is a very "definitive" sound on each chord, this works well with or without a rhythm section:

TRACK 24
piano only

TRACK 25
piano plus
rhythm section

The melody is derived from the G blues and E blues scales (similar to tracks 20 and 21).

Seven-three extended chord voicings

We will now add a third note to the previous seven-three voicings, to create "seven-three extended" voicings. This technique works particularly well on dominant chords in jazz and jazz-blues, as well as in R&B/funk styles. The following are the most commonly used 7–3 extended voicings for dominant chords in jazz and jazz-blues:

TRACK 26

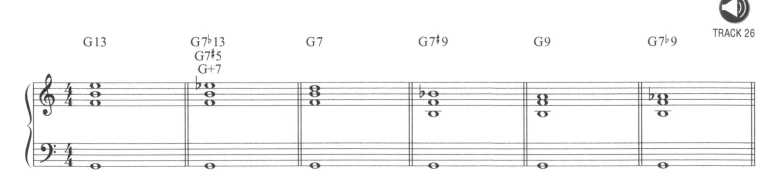

The bottom two notes of the right-hand voicing in each case are the 7th and 3rd of the chord, and above these an extra note has been added. The second measure has some alternate chord symbols provided. We saw earlier that the "+" symbol meant the 5th of the chord was raised, and that the raised 5th was equivalent to the lowered 13th. The three chord symbols in this measure are therefore equivalent to one another.

The previous additions to the basic dominant seven-three voicing can be analyzed as follows:

- In measure 1, the 13th (E) has been added to the basic G7, creating a G13 chord overall.

- In measure 2, the raised 5th or lowered 13th (E♭) has been added to the basic G7, creating a G7#5, G7♭13, or G+7 chord overall.

- In measure 3, the 5th (D) has been added to the basic G7. As this is also a basic chord tone, the resulting chord is still a G7.

- In measure 4, the raised 9th (shown here as B♭, for consistency with the implied key of C minor) has been added to the basic G7, creating a G7#9 chord overall.

- In measure 5, the 9th (A) has been added to the basic G7, creating a G9 chord overall.

- In measure 6, the lowered 9th (A♭) has been added to the basic G7, creating a G7♭9 chord overall.

Next, we will make use of these seven-three extended voicings on a 4-bar jazz-blues progression in C:

TRACK 27
part 1

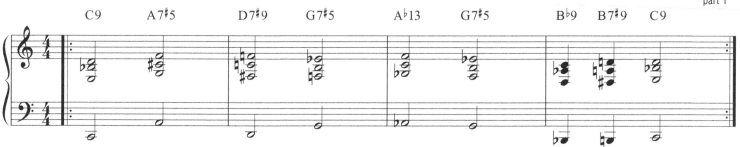

This type of I–VI–II–V progression (first two measures) could be used as an intro or vamp progression in various jazz and jazz-blues styles. The seven-three extended voicings in this example are derived as follows:

- The 9th has been added above the 7th on the C9 in measures 1 and 4, and the B♭9 in measure 4.

- The #5th (♭13th) has been added above the 3rd on the A7#5 in measure 1, and the G7#5 in measures 2 and 3.

- The #9th has been added above the 7th on the D7#9 in measure 2, and the B7#9 in measure 4.

- The 13th has been added above the 3rd on the A♭13 in measure 3.

Now for a jazz-blues rhythmic pattern using the above voicings:

TRACK 27
part 2

This pattern has a sixteenth-note feel and would be suitable for various jazz-rock or R&B styles.

Seven-three extended voicings can also be used in the left hand below a melody or solo, as in the following example:

TRACK 28
piano only

TRACK 29
piano plus
rhythm section

"Double 4th" shapes and chord voicings

Our next voicing technique in this chapter uses what I call "double 4th" shapes. These are three-note voicings created by stacking two perfect 4th intervals on top of one another. I use the term "shape" when referring to these, as (unlike the triad and four-part voicings earlier in this chapter) they are not easily or helpfully described with individual chord symbols. Their interchangeability within different overall chords does, however, make them excellent "upper structure" voicing choices across a range of jazz and pop/R&B styles. In jazz-blues, they are primarily useful in minor keys, and in more modern jazz-rock or jazz-fusion blues. Here are some double-4th-over-root voicings for major, dominant, altered dominant, minor, and suspended dominant chords:

TRACK 30

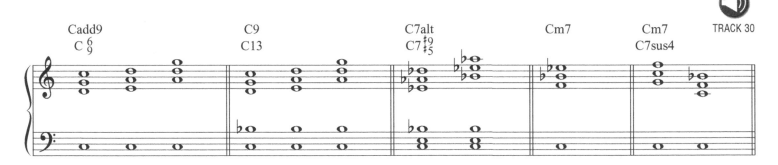

We can analyze the above voicings as follows:

- In measure 1, we are building double 4th shapes from the 9th, 3rd, and 6th of the overall major chord. These upper shapes add various combinations of the 6th and the 9th to the chord.

- In measure 2, we are building double 4th shapes, like in measure 1, but now from the 9th, 3rd and 13th (6th) of the overall dominant chord. The root–7th interval is included in the left hand which helps define the dominant quality. These shapes add various combinations of the 9th and the 13th (6th) to the chord.

- In measure 3, we are building double 4th shapes from the raised 9th and the 7th of the overall altered dominant chord. Note the root-7th-3rd shape in the left hand which helps define the dominant quality. These shapes add various combinations of the ♯9th, ♯5th and the ♭9th to the chord.

- In measure 4, we are building a double 4th shape from the 4th/11th of the overall minor chord. This upper shape adds the 4th/11th to the chord.

- In measure 5, we are building double 4th shapes from the 5th and root of the overall minor or suspended dominant chord (these combinations work for both types of chords). Both of these upper shapes add the 4th/11th to the minor chord.

Although we have used detailed chord symbols in the previous example (to describe the extensions/alterations added with the double 4ths), in practice, the jazz-blues pianist will often use these voicings to upgrade basic major, minor, or dominant chord symbols on a chart. Also note that the inversions and "octave doubling" (repeating the top note of a shape, one octave lower) can be applied to all of the right-hand shapes, as shown previously.

Next we will apply double-4th-over-root voicings to a 12-bar jazz-blues progression in A minor:

On the above minor 7th chords, double 4th shapes have been built from the 4th/11th and 5th in each case. This gives a modern transparent sound, which might then be rhythmically stylized as follows:

This was recorded with a "straight eighths" feel on the audio, and is suitable for a jazz-rock blues in a minor key. Next we will use the same double 4th voicings and rhythms, this time in the left hand to support a jazz-blues melody in the right hand:

The melody in the preceding example is derived from the blues scale built from the tonic (A blues in this case), a typical choice for jazz-blues tunes in minor keys.

Polychord voicings

The last voicing technique to explore in this chapter is "polychords," which is the use of two upper structures simultaneously (one in each hand). In jazz-blues styles, three-note shapes are frequently used (i.e. combinations of triads, 7–3 extended, and double 4ths). This became a staple jazz technique from the 1950s, onward (pioneered by pianists such as Bill Evans and McCoy Tyner), and is also applicable to many jazz-blues tunes. Although many combinations are possible between the hands, the following guidelines can help get you started:

- On dominant chords, the left-hand shape is frequently "7–3 extended," with the 7th and 3rd as the lowest two notes. The right-hand shape is often an upper structure triad, or a double 4th.

- On major and minor chords, using a double 4th shape in the left hand gives a modern and "jazzy" sound. Again, this is often combined with a triad or another double 4th shape in the right hand.

- All of the polychord voicings for dominant chords with the 7th and 3rd on the bottom (measures 3–13 of the following example show some of the possibilities) actually belong to more than one dominant chord. Some of these "alternate" dominant symbols are shown above the staff. For example, in measure 7 the bottom two notes (F and B) are not only the 3rd and 7th of a G7, but also the 7th and 3rd of a Db7. This dual relationship between dominant chords underpins a lot of the chord substitutions and reharmonization found in jazz styles.

Here are some typical jazz-blues polychord voicing combinations, using upper structures we have already identified in this chapter:

TRACK 34

We can further analyze these voicings as follows:

- In measure 1, the Dm7 chord is voiced by building a double 4th shape from the root in the left hand (adding the 4th/11th to the chord), and a major triad from the 3rd in the right hand.

- In measure 2, the Cm7 chord is voiced by building a double 4th shape from the 4th/11th in the left hand, and a double 4th shape from the 5th in the right hand. (Both of these add the 4th/11th to the chord).

- In measure 3, the G13 chord is voiced by building a 7–3 extended shape (7–3–13) from the 7th in the left hand, and a major triad from the root in the right hand.

- In measure 4, the G13 chord is again voiced by building a 7–3 extended shape (7–3–13) from the 7th in the left hand, this time with a minor triad built from the 13th in the right hand.

- In measure 5, the C9 chord is voiced by building a 7–3 extended shape (3–7–9) from the 3rd in the left hand, and a major triad from the root in the right hand.

- In measure 6, the C9 chord is again voiced by building a 7–3 extended shape (3–7–9) from the 3rd in the left hand, this time with a minor triad built from the 5th in the right hand.

- In measure 7, the G7♭5♭9 chord is voiced by building a 7–3 extended shape (7–3–♯5) from the 7th in the left hand, and a major triad from the ♭5th/♯11th in the right hand. As noted, this voicing is also equivalent to a D♭9 chord.

- In measure 8, the G7♯5♯9 chord is voiced by again building a 7–3 extended shape (7–3–♯5) from the 7th in the left hand, this time with a major triad built from the ♯5th/♭13th in the right hand. As noted, this voicing is also equivalent to a D♭9♯11 chord.

- In measure 9, the G7♯5♭9 chord is voiced by again building a 7–3 extended shape (7–3–♯5) from the 7th in the left hand, this time with a minor triad built from the ♭9th in the right hand. As noted, this voicing is also plural to a D♭9 chord.

- In measure 10, the G13 chord is voiced by building a 7–3 extended shape (7–3–13) from the 7th in the left hand, and a double 4th shape from the 9th in the right hand.

- In measure 11, the C13 chord is voiced by building a 7–3 extended shape (3–7–9) from the 3rd in the left hand, and a double 4th shape from the 13th in the right hand.

- In measure 12, the G7alt chord is voiced by building a 7–3 extended shape (7–3–♭13) from the 7th in the left hand, and a double 4th shape from the ♯9th in the right hand (adding the ♯9th, ♯5th/♭13th, and ♭9th to the chord).

- In measure 13, the C7alt chord is voiced by building a 7–3 extended shape (3–7–♯9) from the 3rd in the left hand, and a double 4th shape from the 7th in the right hand (adding the ♯9th, and ♯5th/♭13th to the chord).

Now we'll use some of these voicings on a 24-bar jazz-blues waltz progression:

TRACK 35
part 1

We can further analyze the voicings in the above example as follows:

- In measures 1-2 and 13-14, the G13 chord is voiced by building a 7–3 extended shape (7–3–13) from the 7th in the left hand, and a double 4th shape from the 9th in the right hand.

- In measures 3-4 and 9-10, the C13 chord is voiced by building a 7–3 extended shape (3–7–9) from the 3rd in the left hand, and a double 4th shape from the 13th in the right hand.

- In measures 5-6 and 21, the G13 chord is voiced by building a 7–3 extended shape (7–3–13) from the 7th in the left hand, and a minor triad from the 13th in the right hand.

- In measures 7-8, the G13 chord is voiced by building a 7–3 extended shape (7–3–13) from the 7th in the left hand, and a major triad from the root in the right hand.

- In measure 11, the C13 chord is voiced by building a 7–3 extended shape (3–7–9) from the 3rd in the left hand, and a minor triad from the 5th in the right hand.

- In measure 12, the C13 chord is voiced by building a 7–3 extended shape (3–7–9) from the 3rd in the left hand, and a major triad from the root in the right hand.

- In measures 15-16, the E7♯5♯9 chord is voiced by building a 7–3 extended shape (3–7–♯9) from the 3rd in the left hand, and a major triad from the ♯5th/♭13th in the right hand.

- In measures 17-18, the Am7 chord is voiced by building a double 4th shape from the root in the left hand, and a major triad from the 3rd in the right hand.

36

- In measures 19-20, the D7#5#9 chord is voiced by building a 7–3 extended shape (3–7–#9) from the 3rd in the left hand, and a major triad from the #5th/♭13th in the right hand.

- In measure 22, the E7#5#9 chord is voiced by building a 7–3 extended shape (3–7–#9) from the 3rd in the left hand, and a double 4th shape from the 7th in the right hand.

- In measure 23, the A7#5#9 chord is voiced by building a 7–3 extended shape (7–3–#5) from the 7th in the left hand, and a double 4th shape from the #9th in the right hand.

- In measure 24, the D7#5#9 chord is voiced by building a 7–3 extended shape (3–7–#9) from the 3rd in the left hand, and a double 4th from the #5th/♭13th in the right hand.

Now we can apply a jazz-blues waltz rhythmic pattern to these voicings, as follows:

TRACK 35
part 2
piano only

TRACK 36
piano plus
rhythm section

We'll learn more about jazz-blues waltz rhythms and styles in Chapter 5. In the next chapter we'll take a closer look at the chord progressions and left- and right-hand patterns you'll need to know in order to play authentic jazz-blues on the piano.

Chapter 4

PROGRESSIONS & PATTERNS FOR LEFT & RIGHT HANDS

Jazz-blues chord progressions and form

Most blues styles are organized around a twelve-measure structure or **form**, and jazz-blues is no exception. This means that a twelve-measure chord progression is repeated for both the melody and the improvised solo parts of the song. Simpler jazz-blues tunes will use more basic blues progressions, whereas more sophisticated jazz-blues tunes may use additional chords and substitutions. In this chapter we'll take a look at several chord progressions commonly used in jazz-blues styles.

Progression Example #1 – Basic blues

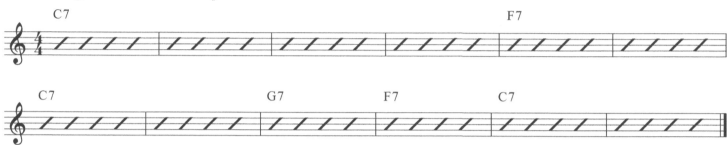

This is the most basic blues progression and form, and is used for a great deal of blues, blues/rock and R&B, as well as for simpler jazz-blues. We can make the following observations about this progression:

* The chords used are dominant 7th chords built from the 1st, 4th and 5th degrees of the key (C Major).

* The 12-bar sequence breaks down into three sections of four bars each, as follows:

    1) The first four bars begin with the dominant 7th built from the 1st degree (C7 in this case).

    2) The second four bars (measures 5–8) begin with the dominant 7th built from the 4th degree (F7 in this case), returning to the dominant 7th built from the 1st degree in bar 7.

    3) The third four bars (9–12) begin with the dominant 7th built from the 5th degree (G7 in this case), followed by the dominant 7th built from the 4th degree in bar 10, and then returning to the dominant 7th built from the 1st degree in bar 11.

Regardless of how simple or sophisticated the progression is, it will be helpful to think of it in four-measure sections as described above. The simplest jazz-blues uses dominant chords only (as in the above example), but the more sophisticated examples will add other chord qualities (such as minor and major chords).

A very common variation on the above progression is to add the IV chord in measure 2 and the V chord in measure 12, as follows:

Progression Example #2 – Variation (a) on basic 12-bar

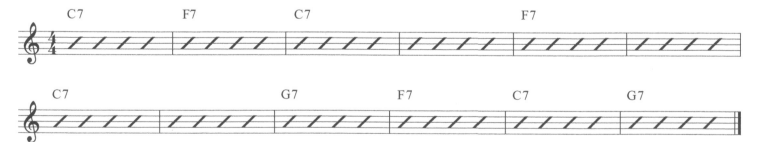

Numerous jazz-blues tunes use these basic progressions and variations. Examples include "Basie's Thought" (Count Basie) and "I Don't Worry" (Mose Allison).

Our next variation adds a II–V progression (chords built from the 2nd and 5th degrees of the key) which is a cornerstone of jazz harmony:

Progression Example #3 – Variation (b) on basic 12-bar

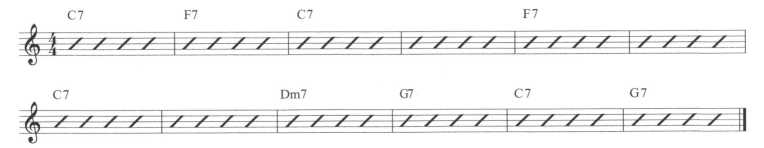

Note the II–V progression (Dm7–G7) in measures 9–10. This progression is used for "Miguel's Party" (Bud Powell), "Kelly's Blues," (Wynton Kelly) and others.

Next we'll add a VI chord (built from the 6th degree) before the II–V chords. Here the VI chord used is an A7 which leads strongly into the following Dm7. (Another option would have been to use an Am7, which is diatonic to the key of C).

Progression Example #4 – Variation (c) on basic 12-bar

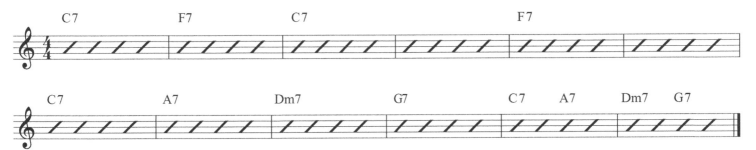

Note the I–VI–II–V sequences in the preceding example, from measures 7–10, and 11–12. Measures 11 and 12 of the blues form are a "turnaround" section, leading back to the top of the form, and present many chord progression possibilities as we shall see. It is not unusual to have a busier "chord rhythm" in the turn-around section—in this case we have four chords in the last two measures, each one lasting for two beats. "Jeep's Blues" (Duke Ellington) is a noted jazz-blues tune which uses this progression.

There are many other possible variations on the 12-bar blues progression, for example:

- using a chord built from the $\flat$VII of the key instead of the tonic chord (i.e., B$\flat$7 instead of C7, on a blues in C) during measures 11–12, as in "Freddie Freeloader" (Miles Davis).

- using a series of substitute changes (i.e., two beats each on E$\flat$7–A$\flat$7–D7–G7, on a blues in C) during measures 9-10, as in "Blues of the Prairies" (Oscar Peterson).

Next we will look at a "bebop" 12-bar blues progression. Bebop progressions are normally much busier, often with two chords per measure, even at faster tempos. Lots of II–V and substitute chords, and different chord qualities (i.e., major, minor, minor 7$\flat$5th etc., as well as dominant) are used, compared to basic blues:

Progression Example #5 – "Bebop" jazz-blues

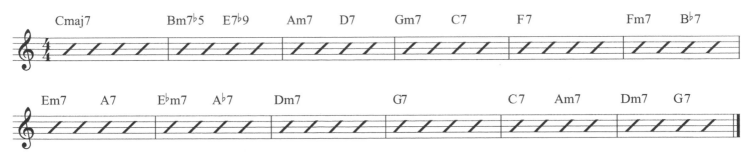

Note that even with this more sophisticated progression, it still makes sense to break it down into 4-measure sections:

- The first four bars still begin with a I or tonic chord in measure 1 (now a major chord instead of a dominant chord).

- The second four bars still begin with a IV chord in measure 5 (still a dominant 7th chord).

- The third four bars begin with a II–V progression in measures 9–10 (a variation on the V chord that we first saw in progression #3).

A number of bebop tunes use this progression, notably "Blues for Alice" (Charlie Parker).

Next we will look at adding more measures to the basic blues form, creating an extra section known as a "tag." Frequently, this consists of a repetition of existing measures from within the form. For example, if we took the basic blues progression and repeated measures 9–10 three times, we would get the following 16-measure form:

Progression Example #6 – Basic blues with "tag" (16 measures)

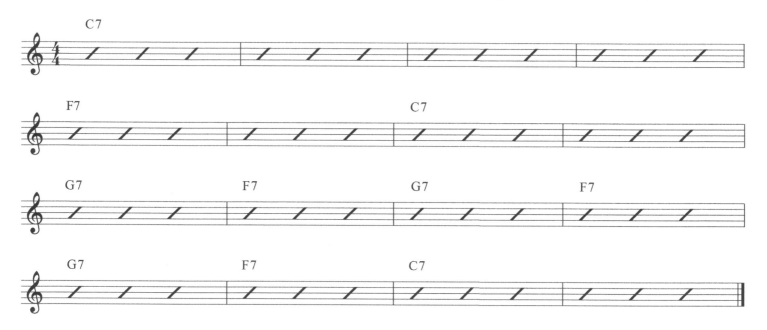

The G7–F7 is repeated three times, before the C7 chord in measure 15. A famous example of this type of "blues with a tag" would be the Herbie Hancock tune "Watermelon Man."

Many jazz-blues tunes will also use 12-bar "minor" blues progressions. In this case, the I and IV chords are typically minor 7ths instead of dominant 7ths. The V chord is still normally a dominant 7th, often preceeded by the dominant built from the $\flat$VI (lowered 6th of the key) in measure 9 of the form, as follows:

Progression Example #7 – "Minor" blues

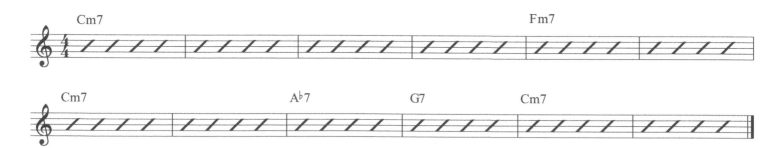

Noted examples of jazz-blues tunes using these changes include "Equinox" (John Coltrane) and "Twelve Inch" (Curtis Fuller).

Jazz-blues "waltz" tunes often use similar chord changes, but over a 24-measure form in $\frac{3}{4}$ time. Here is an example of a jazz-blues waltz form:

Progression Example #8 — "Minor" blues waltz (24 measures)

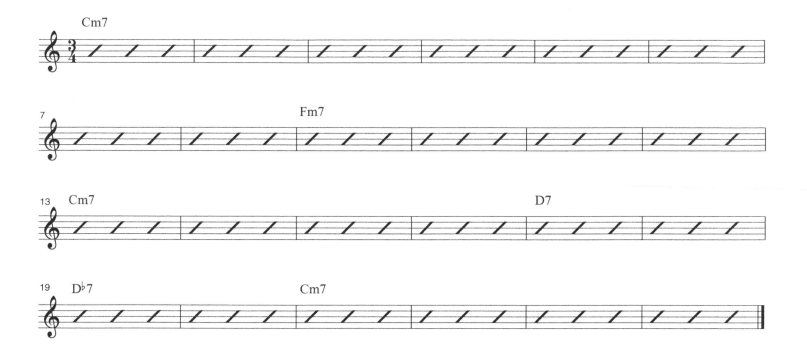

"Footprints" by Wayne Shorter is a noted example of a minor jazz-blues waltz using these changes.

As with other blues forms, there are various chord substitutions possible in the jazz-blues waltz. Measures 17-20 can be varied as follows:

- F#m7♭5, B7alt, Em7♭5, A7alt (one chord per measure)—also used for "Footprints."
- G7#9 (2 measures), A♭7#9, G7#9 (one measure each)—used for "All Blues" (Miles Davis).

Jazz-blues patterns

Now we look at the left-hand and right-hand patterns commonly used in different jazz-blues styles. Each of the following examples is a specific combination of left- and right-hand techniques, applied to a 12-bar blues progression. You are encouraged to practice these hands separately and together, and also "mix and match" left- and right-hand parts from different examples to create your own combinations.

Each of these examples has a "piano only" track on the play-along audio, with the left hand part on the left channel, the right hand part on the right channel, and the hi-hat quarter-note click in the middle. This enables you to practice these examples "hands separately," by turning down one channel or the other. Some examples also have a second track, with a jazz-blues rhythm section on the left channel, and the piano part (left and right hands) on the right channel. To play along with the band on these examples, turn down the right channel.

Pattern #1 – Left-hand stride style, right-hand octaves

Our first pattern combination (in the style of Fats Waller or Count Basie) features a left-hand "stride style" pattern and right-hand octaves, using chord progression example #4:

In this example, the left-hand "stride style" involves playing the root, root–7th, or root–10th (3rd) of each chord on beat 1 of each measure, followed by a chord voicing (typically four-part) on beat 2. If the chord lasts for the whole measure, the left hand normally plays the 5th of the chord on beat 3, followed by another chord voicing on beat 4. Don't worry if you can't stretch the root–10th intervals in the left hand. Just play the root of the chord instead. Sometimes, this overall pattern will be varied with a chromatic walkup, as in measure 4 of this example. Again, just play the lowest note of each interval if you have a problem stretching the 10ths.

On the dominant chords, the left-hand voicings on beats 2 and 4 are all either basic dominant 7th shapes built from the root of the dominant chord, or minor $7^{\flat}5$ shapes built from the 3rd. The Dm7 chord is voiced with the basic minor 7th shape built from the root.

The right-hand octave figures often have a middle note in between the outer notes, resulting in a three-note shape, sometimes referred to as a "filled in" octave. The top note most frequently used is C, which is typical, as this is a blues progression in C (the two most common repeated notes over a blues progression would be either the tonic or 5th degree of the key, i.e., C or G in this case). The middle note is normally a chord tone of the current chord. In the first measure the middle note is G (the 5th of the C7), which moves to A (the 3rd of the F7) in measure 2, and so on.

In measure 4 we have an octave phrase without the middle note. This is from the A blues scale (a common scale source on a blues in C, as A is the relative minor of C). On the A7–Dm7–G7 progression in measures 8–10 and 11–12, note that the right-hand top line moves by half steps to voice lead through the 7ths and 3rds of these chords, a classic jazz piano technique. Rhythmically, note the use of eighth-note anticipations in the right hand (anticipating beats 2 and 4 in measure 1, beat 3 in measure 2, etc). This is very effective when combined with the steady quarter-note pulse in the left hand.

Pattern #2 – Left-hand jump blues ostinato, right-hand blues scales and drones

The next pattern (in the style of Oscar Peterson) combines a single-note left-hand pattern reminiscent of jump blues and boogie-woogie, with right-hand phrases using blues scales and "drones." This pattern uses chord progression example #1:

In this example, the left hand is playing an eighth note pattern using the 1–5–6–5–7–5–6–5 of each chord (note the "7" signifies a minor 7th above the root, as these are all dominant 7th chords). This is a common jump blues pattern and imparts a lot of energy to the rhythm.

The right hand is using "drone" phrases from the C and A blues scales (A being the relative minor of C). Here a "drone" is defined as a repeated or held note, above changing notes/intervals below. For example, in measures 1–2 the drone of C is repeated above the moving line of G–Gb–F–Eb–E. This is a signature sound across the range of blues and jazz-blues styles. The most common drone notes are the tonic of the key (C in this case, used in measures 1–2, 5–6, and 9–10), and the minor 7th interval above the tonic (Bb in this case, used in measures 3–4, 7–8, and 11–12).

Pattern #3 – Left-hand "root-7th" bop style, right-hand triads

The next pattern (in the style of Bud Powell or Thelonious Monk) combines root–7th, root–7th–3rd and root–3rd–7th shapes in the left hand, with upper structure triads in the right hand. This pattern uses chord progression example #3 (varied by staying on the C7 chord during measures 11–12):

In this example, both hands are "locked together" playing the syncopated figures. The rhythms are based on a two-measure phrase, landing on beat 1 and the "and" of 2 (halfway through beat 2) in the first measure, and on the "and" of 1 and on beat 3 in the second measure. This rhythmic phrasing is common in mainstream jazz and swing styles. (More about rhythmic "counting" and subdivisions in Chapter 5.)

The left hand is playing root–7th intervals (measure 9), root–7th–3rd shapes (measures 2, 5–6, and 10), or root–3rd–7th shapes (measures 1, 3–4, 7–8, and 11–12). These voicings can sound "muddy" if played too low on the piano—let your ears be the judge when you use them.

The right hand is using upper structure triads on all of the dominant chords, moving between minor triads built from the 5th (i.e., Gm on the C7 chord) and from the 13th (i.e., Am on the C7 chord). The Dm7 is voiced by building a major triad from the 3rd: F/Dm7.

Pattern #4 – Left-hand block chords, right-hand Mixolydian thirds

The next pattern (in the style of Red Garland) combines block (or four-part) shapes in the left hand, with third intervals and single-note phrases from Mixolydian modes in the right hand, using chord progression example #3:

TRACK 41
piano only

TRACK 42
piano plus
rhythm section

The steady quarter-note pulse in the left hand makes this setting suitable for ballads and slower-tempo blues tunes. The voicings used on the dominant chords are combinations of basic dominant 7th shapes, minor 7♭5th shapes built from the 3rd (i.e., Em7♭5 on the C7 chord), and major 7♭5th shapes built from the 7th (i.e., B♭maj7♭5 on the C7 chord). The top notes of these voicings create a slow moving counterpoint to the right-hand phrases. The Dm7 is voiced by building a major 7th shape from the 3rd (Fmaj7 on the Dm7 chord, resulting in a Dm9, overall), and by building a basic minor 7th shape from the root.

The right-hand part is derived from Mixolydian modes built from the root of each dominant chord (i.e., C Mixolydian over the C7, F Mixolydian over the F7, etc.). So the thirds in measure 1, 3–4, 8 and 11, all come from C Mixolydian (review track 9 in Chapter 3, if needed). Similarly, the third intervals in measure 5 come from the F Mixolydian mode. The single-note phrase used in measures 2, 6 and 10, can also be found in the A blues scale (A being the relative minor of C).

Although this pattern could be used for accompaniment on a jazz-blues ballad, note that there is still a melodic or "linear" character to the right-hand part. This illustrates the blurred line that exists in many blues and jazz-blues styles between accompaniment (or "comping") and melody/solo treatments.

Pattern #5 – Left-hand single-note "in 2," right-hand Mixolydian triads

The next pattern (in the style of Count Basie or Oscar Peterson) combines a single-note part "in 2" (landing on beats 1 and 3 of each measure) in the left hand, with triad shapes and some third intervals from Mixolydian modes in the right hand, using chord progression example #2:

TRACK 43

In this example, the left hand is playing an eighth-note "pickup," leading into beats 1 and/or 3 of each measure. Normally, the root of the chord is played on beat 1, with another chord tone (most often the 5th) being played on beat 3. The eighth-note "pickups" can be repeated chord tones, adjacent scale tones, or half-step movements. This is essentially creating a bass part, and is therefore suitable for solo piano applications.

The right-hand triads are derived from Mixolydian modes built from the root of each dominant chord (i.e., C Mixolydian over the C7, F Mixolydian over the F7, etc.). So, the Gm, F, E° and Dm triads in measure 1 all come from C Mixolydian (review track 10 in Chapter 3, if needed). Similarly, the Cm (anticipating beat 1) and Dm triads in measure 2 come from the F Mixolydian mode. Some Mixolydian thirds are also used, alternating with the thumb playing the root on upbeats as in measures 5, 7, and 9. Also note that half-step grace notes are used to lead into the 3rds and/or 5ths of the dominant chords (in measures 1, 2, 5, 7, 9, and 10).

Pattern #6 – Left-hand single-note "in 4," right-hand "7-3" extended voicings

Next up is a pattern (in the style of Mose Allison) combining a single-note part "in 4" (landing on all four downbeats of each measure) in the left hand, with 7–3 extended voicings in the right hand. This uses a variation on chord progression example #4, with dominant 7#9th chords built from the tonic (measures 1 and 3) and altered dominants (either with #5th or #9th) used on the I–VI–II–V progression in measures 7–10 and 11-12, as follows:

This type of left-hand part (landing on all four downbeats of each measure) is sometimes referred to as a "walking bass" style. There are many ways to construct a walking bass line over jazz-blues chord changes, but these general guidelines will help:

- The root of the chord is almost always played on beat 1 of each measure, except when a chord change is continuing into a second measure. In this case, other basic chord tones (3rd, 5th or 7th) can be used on beat 1 of the second measure.

- Once you know what register you want to play the root of the next chord in (i.e., how high or low) you can then design an ascending or descending line during the preceding measure to lead into that root note. These lines often use scale-wise movement (Mixolydian modes) or chordal arpeggios (triads or dominant 7th chords).

- Successive ascending or descending half-step intervals are often used, for example connecting the 3rd to the 5th of a chord (3, 4, ♯4, 5) or the 7th to the 5th (♭7, 6, ♭6, 5).

- A half-step interval is often used between beat 4 of a measure and the root of the next chord on beat 1 of the following measure. This kind of half-step approach is especially common in jazz-blues.

With these guidelines in mind, let's take a closer look at how the walking bass line in the preceding example was constructed:

- From measure 1 to measure 2 we descend scale-wise from C to F, using the C Mixolydian scale.

- In measure 2 after the F on beat 1, we ascend chromatically from the 3rd of the F7 (A, B♭, B) to lead back into the C needed on the next chord.

- In measure 3 we ascend chromatically from the 9th of the C7 up to the 3rd (D, E♭, E), before playing the 5th (G) as an eighth-note pickup into the next measure.

- From measure 4 to measure 5 we again descend scale-wise from C to F, using the C Mixolydian mode.

- In measure 5 we ascend using arpeggiated chord tones of the F7 chord (1–3–5–6).

- In measure 6 after the F on beat 1, we descend chromatically from the 7th of the F7 (E♭, D, D♭), to lead back into the C needed on the next chord.

- In measure 7 we descend using the root, 7th and 5th of the C7 (C, B♭, G) before ascending in half-steps to lead into the A needed on the next chord.

- In measure 8 we ascend and then descend using arpeggiated chord tones of the altered A7 chord (1–3–#5–♭5). The last E♭ also leads into the D needed on the next chord, by half-step.

- In measure 9 we descend using altered chord tones of the D7 chord (1–7–#5–♭5). The last A♭ also leads into the G needed on the next chord, by half-step.

- In measure 10 we ascend and then descend using arpeggiated chord tones of the altered G7 chord (1–3–#5–♭5). The last D♭ also leads into the C needed on the next chord, by half-step.

- In measures 11–12 we have a busier chord rhythm (two chords per measure) typical of turnaround sections, leading back to the top of the form. Here we have the root of each chord on beats 1 and 3, and a half-step approach to the next chord root on beats 2 and 4. Notice that the last note, D♭, provides for a half-step approach, back to the beginning.

The right-hand voicings on these dominant chords are all 7–3 extended, as follows:

- On the C7#9 chords in measures 1, 3–4, 7 and 11, and the D7#9 chords in measures 9 and 12, the voicing is 3–7–#9 (from bottom to top).

- On the F7 chords in measures 2, and 5–6, the voicing is 7–3–13 (from bottom to top).

- On the A7#5 chords in measures 8 and 11, and the G7#5 chords in measures 10 and 12, the voicing is 7–3–#5 (from bottom to top).

Again, note the eighth-note anticipations used in the right hand, in particular the anticipations of beat 1 leading into chord changes (on the last eighth note of measures 1, 4, 6, 9 and 11).

Pattern #7 – Left-hand "7-3" voicings, right-hand "double 4th" shapes

The next pattern (in the style of Bill Evans) combines 7-3 voicings in the left hand, with double 4th shapes in the right hand, using chord progression example #2 (varied by staying on the C7 chord during measures 11–12):

TRACK 45
piano only

TRACK 46
piano plus
rhythm section

Rhythmically, this example is similar to pattern #3 (tracks 39/40), in that both hands are "locked together" when playing the syncopated figures. The left hand is playing the 7–3 of each dominant, in the area just below middle C which is the best register for these voicings. The right hand is playing double 4th shapes, built from the 9th and 3rd of the C7, and the 13th of the F7 and G7 chords. The resulting five-note shapes between the hands impart a transparent and modern flavor to this jazz-blues pattern.

Pattern #8 — Left-hand "7-3" extended voicings, right-hand triads

Our final pattern in this chapter (also in the style of Bill Evans) combines 7–3 extended voicings in the left hand, with upper structure triads in the right hand, creating "polychord" combinations between the hands (review track 34 in Chapter 3, as needed). This example uses the same chord progression and rhythms as the previous pattern #7:

The left hand is playing 7–3 extended voicings on all the dominant chords: 3–7–9 on the C7 chord, and 7–3–13 and 7–3–5 on the F7 and G7 chords. The right-hand triads are a mix of basic major triads built from the root, and minor triads built from the 5th (i.e., Gm/C7) and 13th (i.e., Dm/F7). The resulting poly-chords are all staple sounds across a range of mainstream jazz and jazz-blues styles.

Chapter 5
JAZZ-BLUES STYLES and COMPING

In this chapter we will develop a range of jazz-blues "comping" (or accompaniment) styles as used by some important jazz-blues pianists and stylistic innovators. We will build on the various left-hand and right-hand patterns shown in the last chapter, by combining multiple techniques in either or both hands, and applying them to longer progressions and examples.

Rhythmic concepts

As noted earlier, most jazz-blues uses a **swing eighths** rhythmic subdivision or feel. However, with the development of jazz-rock and fusion (beginning in the late 60s/70s), other rhythms such as straight eighths and straight sixteenths began to emerge. We will now review these different rhythmic subdivisions.

In straight eighths, each eighth note is of equal length and divides the beat exactly in half, as follows:

Straight eighth notes

TRACK 49

Note the rhythmic counting below the staff—this is how eighth note rhythms are normally counted, with the 1, 2, 3, and 4 falling on the **downbeats**, and the "&s" falling halfway in between, on the **upbeats**.

In a swing eighths feel, the second eighth note in each beat (the "&" in the rhythmic counting) lands two-thirds of the way through the beat. This is equivalent to playing on the first and third parts of an eighth-note triplet. We still count using "1 & 2 &" etc., but now each "&" is played a little later:

Swing eighth notes

TRACK 50

Note that the first measure above looks the same as the previous straight eighths example, but when a swing eighths interpretation is applied to it, it sounds equivalent to the second measure above (the quarter-eighth triplets). However, as the second measure above is more cumbersome to write and to read, it is common practice to notate as in the first measure above, but to rhythmically interpret in a swing-eighths style as needed. This is common practice across a range of mainstream jazz and jazz-blues styles.

In a jazz-blues waltz (notated in $\frac{3}{4}$ time, as in tracks 35/36), it is also normal for the eighth notes to be treated as swing eighths.

There will also be times when we need to land on all three parts of an eighth-note triplet. In this case, the swing eighths rhythmic interpretation will not work, as this only allows us to access the first and third parts of the triplet. Instead, we either need to use eighth-note triplet signs in $\frac{4}{4}$ (or $\frac{3}{4}$) time, or use $\frac{12}{8}$ (or $\frac{9}{8}$) time which "exposes" all of the eighth notes without the need for triplet signs. The following example shows $\frac{4}{4}$ time with eighth-note triplets, compared with $\frac{12}{8}$ time:

Eighth-note triplets vs. $\frac{12}{8}$ time

TRACK 51

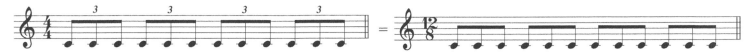

In the first measure above, each beat is divided into three equal parts. In the second measure, the time signature allows for twelve eighth notes in the measure, but we still subjectively hear four "big beats" at the start of each beamed group of eighth notes. The two measures above are therefore functionally equivalent to one another. As a general rule, I would suggest notating in $\frac{4}{4}$ time unless there are a lot of eighth-note triplet signs needed, when it may be less cumbersome to notate in $\frac{12}{8}$ time.

In a straight-sixteenths feel, each sixteenth note is of equal length and divides the eighth-note exactly in half (and the beat exactly into quarters) as follows:

Straight sixteenth notes

TRACK 52

Again, note the rhythmic counting below the staff—this is how sixteenth note rhythms are normally counted. In between the beat numbers (1, 2, 3, 4) and the "&s," we have the "e" on the 2nd sixteenth note within each beat, and the "a" on the 4th sixteenth note within each beat.

Now we will begin looking at various jazz-blues comping styles for the piano. The play-along audio contains two tracks for most of these examples. The first track is piano only, with the left-hand part on the left channel, the right-hand part on the right channel, and the hi-hat quarter-note click in the middle. This enables you to practice these examples hands separately, by turning down one channel or the other. The second track has a jazz-blues rhythm section on the left channel, and the piano part (left and right hands) on the right channel. To play along with the band on these examples, turn down the right channel.

Comping Style #1 – Medium swing (Gene Harris)

Our first comping example in this chapter has a medium swing feel, and is in the style of Gene Harris, (an important soul-jazz pianist from the 1960s, onward). The first 12-bar section features Mixolydian thirds and blues scale figures in the right hand, over root–7ths (and a root–3rd–7th shape on the D7 chord) in the left hand. The second 12-bar section features blues scale drone phrases and Mixolydian triads in the right hand, over 7–3 extended voicings in the left hand. This blues progression is in G, and is based on example #2 from Chapter 4:

TRACK 53
piano only

TRACK 54
piano plus
rhythm section

In the first 12-bar section, the right hand is playing 3rds from the G and C Mixolydian modes (in measures 1–8 and 11–12), as well as some chromatically ascending and descending intervals (3rds and 6ths). In measures 9–10, drone-note phrases and fills are used from the G blues scale, and also from the E blues scale during beat 4 of measure 10 (E being the relative minor of G). Meanwhile, the left hand is playing root–7th intervals on all of the dominant chords, with the root–3rd–7th variation on the D7 chord in measure 9.

In the second 12-bar section, the right hand is playing more drone note phrases from the G blues scale, starting with the tonic of the scale (G) as the drone in measures 13-14, 17, 19 and 23, and using the ♭7th of the scale (F) as the drone in measures 15 and 18. Descending triads from the G Mixolydian mode are also used in measures 16 and 19–20, with the Em and Dm triads "linked" with the chromatic passing triad of E♭m (this is also a favorite device in gospel styles). On the ending phrase in measure 24, double 4th shapes are built from the 3rd of the A♭7 and G7 chords (upgrading these chords to dominant 13ths). Meanwhile, the left hand is playing 7-3 extended voicings on all of the dominant chords except for the root–7th intervals in measure 24.

Note that the busier and more melodic nature of this example (particularly the second chorus) would make it suitable for a melody and/or solo treatment. As previously discussed, there is often no clear division between comping styles and melody/solo styles when playing blues or jazz-blues.

Comping Style #2 – Swing/stride combination (Oscar Peterson)

The next comping example is also at a medium tempo, and combines some swing, jump blues and stride elements in the style of Oscar Peterson, a noted pianist and innovator in a range of jazz and jazz-blues styles. The first 12-bar section features third and sixth intervals and arpeggiated figures in the right hand, over an ostinato (repeated pattern) in the left hand, reminiscent of jump blues and boogie-woogie styles. The second 12-bar section features Mixolydian thirds, blues scale "drone" phrases and octaves with grace notes in the right hand, over more ostinatos, followed by "stride" voicings in the left hand. F is the key for this blues progression based on example #2, from Chapter 4, with various substitutions added:

TRACK 55

Note the chord substitutions used in measures 9–10 (A♭7–D♭7–G7–C7) and the variation in measures 21–22, all typical Oscar Peterson harmonic techniques. Also, the chord changes in measures 23–24 are a commonly used ending in various blues and jazz-blues styles.

In the first 12-bar section, the right hand is playing a chromatically descending series of sixth intervals (i.e., C up to A, B up to A♭, B♭ up to G, etc., in measure 1) on the dominant chords, alternating with Mixolydian and chromatic third intervals. Over the extra substitute chords in measures 9–10, the right hand is playing an arpeggiated figure using chord tones, ending on the 7–3 of the C7 chord (on the "and" of two). Meanwhile, the left hand is playing an eighth-note pattern using the 1–5–6–5–7–5–6–5 of each chord, varied for the busier chord rhythm in measures 9–10.

In the second 12-bar section, the right hand is playing a series of Mixolydian thirds (and some fourths) on the F7 chord, except in measure 20, which contains drone-note phrases from the F blues scale. The octave phrases and grace notes over the B♭7 chord in measures 17–18, and over the A♭7–D♭7–G7♯5–C7♯9 chords in measures 21–22, also come from the F blues scale (and are targeting the 3rds and 7ths of the chords in measures 21–22). Meanwhile, the left hand is playing a different ostinato from the first chorus (now using the 1–3–4–♯4–5–6 of each chord), before switching to a stride style in measures 21–22. Varying the left-hand pattern part way through a blues chorus in this manner is another typical Oscar Peterson solo piano device.

Comping Style #3 – Jump blues (Big Joe Turner)

The next comping example is a jump blues in the style of Big Joe Turner, and is also reminiscent of some of the New Orleans blues styles (as played by Fats Domino). As it has an "eighth-note triplet" feel and frequently uses all the parts of each implied triplet, this example has been notated in $\frac{12}{8}$ time to avoid having to write a lot of triplet signs (see track 51 and accompanying text).

The first 12-bar section features upper structure and Mixolydian triads in the right hand, over a typical jump blues ostinato pattern in the left hand. The second 12-bar section then features "crossover" licks, blues scale "drone" phrases, and some Mixolydian thirds in the right hand, over the same ostinato pattern continued in the left hand. This blues progression is in E and is again based on example #2 from Chapter 4:

In the first 12-bar section, the right-hand part in the odd-numbered measures is based on diminished upper structure triads built from the 3rd of each dominant chord, i.e., G#° over the E7, C#° over the A7, and D#° over the B7. Note the ♭3–3 movement of these dominant chords between beats 1–2 and 7–8 of the 12/8 measures. On the A7 in measure 2, the right-hand part is based on the 3–7–9 of the chord (which could be considered an incomplete four-part upper structure built from the 3rd), this time with a 13–♭7 movement occurring between beats 1–2 and 7–8. Elsewhere in the even-numbered measures, we are using Mixolydian triads and more ♭3–3 movements on the dominant chords. Meanwhile, the left hand is playing a simple 1–5–6–♭7–6–5 ostinato pattern, anticipating beat 7 of each 12/8 measure.

In the second 12-bar section, the right hand is playing a series of "crossover" licks in measures 13–15, 17, 19, 21, and 23. "Crossover" licks are an essential ingredient in various blues styles, and are also found in jazz-blues. Most of these crossovers start with the 5th of the chord played in octaves, followed by a rapid descending arpeggio of the chord, leading to the root of the chord being played as a "drone" above the 4th, ♭3rd, and finally the 3rd with respect to the chord. (A variation occurs in measure 14, where the crossover starts with the 9th of the A7 chord played in octaves). The term "crossover" arises because after the descending arpeggio has been played, the upper fingers of the right hand need to "cross over" the thumb on their way to the lower notes in the phrase. Elsewhere the right hand is playing some blues scale drone phrases into measures 16, 18, 20, and 22, using both the E and A blues scales. The left hand is continuing the ostinato pattern established during the first chorus.

For more information on the different types of "crossovers" found in blues styles, please check out my companion volume in this series, *Blues Piano* (also published by Hal Leonard Corporation).

Comping Style #4 – Up-tempo bop blues (Charlie Parker)

The next comping example is a "bop" or bebop jazz-blues at a faster tempo, in the style of Charlie Parker and pianists such as Bud Powell and Erroll Garner, who were active during this period. The first 12-bar section features triad and four-part upper structures in the right hand, over root-7th intervals in the left hand. The second 12-bar section uses polychord voicings between the hands, with the right hand playing upper structure triads and the left hand playing 7–3 extended and double 4th voicings. This blues progression is in F and is based on example #5 from Chapter 4:

TRACK 58
piano only

TRACK 59
piano plus
rhythm section

Note the busier chord progression in this example, with a lot of II–V and substitute chords added, all typical of the bebop period. In the first 12-bar section, the right hand is mostly playing upper structure triads, with some use of four part shapes, as follows:

- The Fmaj7 chords are voiced by building minor 7th four-part chords from the 3rd: Am7/F. These voicings add the 9th to the chord.

- The Em7♭5 chord is voiced by building a minor triad from the 3rd: Gm/E.

- The A7♭9 chord is voiced by building a major 7♭5th four-part chord from the 3rd (C♯maj7♭5/A), moving to a minor triad built from the ♭9th (B♭m/A7). These voicings add the ♯5th and ♯9th to the chord.

- The minor 7th chords are voiced in one of the following ways:
  - building a major triad from the 3rd (F/D, E♭/C etc.).
  - building a major 7th four-part chord from the 3rd (D♭maj7/B♭, Bmaj7/A♭), which adds the 9th to the chord.

- The other dominant 7th chords are voiced in one of the following ways:
  - building a minor triad from the 13th (Em/G7, Dm/F7 etc), adding the 13th to the chord.
  - building a minor triad from the 5th (Am/D7), adding the 9th to the chord.
  - building a major triad from the root (C/C7).
  - building a major 7#5th four-part chord from the 7th (Bmaj7#5/D♭), adding the #11th and 13th.

The left hand is playing root–7th voicings, with use of root–5th (on the Em7♭5) and root–3rd (on the D7).

In the second 12-bar section, the right hand continues to play upper structure triads (sometimes doubling the top note an octave lower), now in a higher register to allow room for the left hand to play 7–3 extended and double 4th voicings around middle C. This combination between the hands creates "polychord" voicings. The right hand voicings are similar to those used in the first chorus. Exceptions include the F major triad built from the root of the Fmaj7 chord in measure 13 and 25, the F and E♭ major triads built from the #5th and ♭5th of the A7♭9 chord in measure 14, and the E♭ major triad built from the 9th of the D♭7 chord in measure 20.

The left hand voicings can be analyzed as follows:

- The Fmaj7 chords are voiced by building double 4th shapes from the 3rd, which adds the 6th and 9th to the chord.

- The minor 7th chords are voiced by building double 4th shapes from the root or from the 5th, adding the 4th/11th.

- The dominant 7th chords are all voiced using 7–3 extended: 7–3–#5 on the A7♭9, 7–3–13 on the G7 and B♭7, and 3–7–9 on the others.

- Note the E–B♭–D voicing used in the left hand, on the Em7♭5 chord in measure 14. This looks like a 7–3 extended shape (same as the 3–7–9 used on the C7 in measure 22), but here it is built from the root of the Em7♭5 chord.

Comping Style #5 – Medium blues waltz (Miles Davis)

The next comping example is a medium blues waltz (in $\frac{3}{4}$ time), in the style of Miles Davis and pianists such as Wynton Kelly and Bill Evans. The blues waltz form is typically 24 measures—twice the number of measures in a normal $\frac{4}{4}$ blues form. The first 24-bar section features Mixolydian triads, as well as some four-part and double 4th upper structures in the right hand. These are placed over various intervals (3rds, 5ths, 6ths and 7ths) built from the root in the left hand. The second 24-bar section uses polychord voicings between the hands, with the right hand playing upper structure triads and double 4th shapes, and the left hand playing 7–3 extended and also some double 4th shapes. This progression is in G, and has a similar form to example #8 from Chapter 4 (but using dominant 7th chords):

TRACK 60
piano only

TRACK 61
piano plus
rhythm section

In the first 24-bar section, the right hand is playing triads from the G and C Mixolydian modes (in measures 1–16 and 21–24), and some four-part and double 4th upper structures in measures 17–20, as follows:

- The Eb13#11 chord is voiced by building a major 7#5th four-part chord from the 7th (Dbmaj7#5/Eb).

- The D7#5#9 chord is voiced by building a double 4th shape from the 7th. (For both of the above voicings, the addition of the 3rd in the left hand helps define the dominant quality).

- The Ab13 chord is voiced by building a major 7b5th four-part chord from the 7th (Gbmaj7b5/Ab).

In measure 24, the fill leading into the next chorus is derived from the E blues scale (E being the relative minor of G).

In measures 1–16 and 21–24, the left hand is playing the root of the chord every two measures, and a moving line above, consisting of the 5th, 13th (6th), 7th, and root of each dominant chord, matching the top notes and rhythms of the Mixolydian triads played by the right hand. In measures 17–20, the left hand is playing root-3rd intervals, supporting the upper-structure voicings in the right hand.

In the second 24-bar section, more substitute and passing chords have been added. The right hand is playing upper structure triads and double 4th shapes in a higher register to allow room for the left hand to play 7–3 extended and double 4th voicings around middle C, creating "polychord" voicings. The right hand voicings can be analyzed as follows:

- The dominant 13th chords (G13, Ab13) are voiced either by building a minor triad from the 13th (Em/G7), or by building a double 4th shape from the 9th. Double 4th shapes built from the 3rd and 13th of the G13 chord are also "overlapped" to create a four-note shape in the last measure. Don't worry if you can't stretch this span in the right hand—just play the top three notes (as in the previous measure).

- The suspended dominant 9th chord (G9sus) is voiced by building a major triad from the 7th (F/G).

- The dominant 9th chords (C9, Db9) are voiced by building a double 4th shape from the 9th. Minor triads built from the 13th and 5th, and a major triad built from the root, are also used on the C9 chord in measures 35–36.

- The Eb13#11 chord in measures 41–42 is voiced by alternating between inversions of F and Eb major triads, built from the 9th and root of the chord, respectively.

- The D7#5#9 chord in measures 43–44 is voiced by alternating between inversions of Bb and Ab major triads, built from the #5th and b5th of the chord, respectively.

The left-hand voicings can be analyzed as follows:

- The dominant 7th chords in measures 25–40 and 45–49 are voiced using 7-3 extended: 7–3–13 on the G13 and Ab13, and 3–7–9 on the C9 and Db9.

- The suspended dominant 9th chord (G9sus, measures 25, 29, 37, and 45) is voiced by building a double 4th shape from the root.

- The Eb13#11 and D7#5#9 chords in measures 41–44 are voiced using root–3rd–7th shapes, providing good definition below the "alternating" triad voicings in the right hand (see above comments).

Comping Style #6 – Jazz-rock minor blues (Horace Silver)

The next comping example is a jazz-rock minor blues using a straight-eighths rhythmic feel, in the style of Horace Silver or Herbie Hancock. Straight-eighths (and straight-sixteenths) rhythmic subdivisions were incorporated into jazz and jazz-blues styles as the fusion era emerged. The first 12-bar section in this example uses Dorian triads in the right hand (appropriate for this minor blues progression), over a left-hand single-note figure using eighth-note anticipations. The second 12-bar section continues with the Dorian triads in the right hand, over fourth intervals and double 4th shapes in the left hand, emphasizing the syncopations by playing the same rhythms in both hands. This blues progression is in G minor and is based on example #7 from Chapter 4, with substitutions added in measures 9–10:

In the first 12-bar section, the right hand is playing Dorian triads on the Gm7 and Cm7 chords: B♭ and C major triads from the G Dorian mode over the Gm7 chord, and E♭ and F major triads from the C Dorian mode over the Cm7 chord. The A7#5#9 in measure 9 is voiced with a four-part major 7♭5th shape built from the 3rd (C#maj7♭5/A), and the A♭9 in measure 10 utilizes a 7–3 extended (3–7–9) voicing. Meanwhile, the left hand is playing a syncopated single-note figure based on chord tones of the minor 7th and dominant chords, adding a root–7th interval on the A♭9 chord in measure 10.

In the second 12-bar section, the right hand continues to play Dorian triads over the minor 7th chords in measures 13–20 and 23–24, in a higher register to make room for the left hand voicings. Otherwise, the right hand upper structures are derived as follows:

- The A7#5#9 chord in measure 21 is voiced by building a major triad from the #5th: F/A7.
- The A♭9 chord in measure 22 is voiced by building a major triad from the 9th: B♭/A♭7.
- The D7#5#9 chord in measure 24 is voiced by building a double 4th shape from the 7th.
- The Gm7 chord in measure 25 is voiced by building a major 7th four-part chord from the 3rd: B♭maj7/G.

Meanwhile, the left hand is playing 4th intervals built from the root of the Gm7 chord in measures 13–16 and 19–20. Together with the bottom notes in the right hand triads, these also create double 4th shapes—so the resulting five-note voicings between the hands could be thought of as a double 4th shape (on the bottom) "overlapping" with a triad shape (on the top), i.e., the middle note is common to both shapes. Elsewhere, the left hand is building a double 4th shape from the 5th of the Cm7 chord in measures 17–18, and from the root of the Gm7 chord in measure 25. On the dominant chords, we are using 7–3 extended voicings: 7–3–#5 on the A7#5#9, 7–3–13 on the A♭9, and 3–7–#9 on the D7#5#9. All of these left-hand shapes create polychords when combined with the right-hand upper structure triads. Also note that the voicings on the Gm7 chords in measures 13, 15 and 19, and on the Cm7 chord in measure 17, move up "in parallel" by whole-step and then back down again, a device borrowed from modal jazz styles.

Comping Style #7 – Jazz-fusion blues (George Duke)

Our last comping example in this chapter is a jazz-fusion blues in the style of George Duke and Jeff Lorber, showing a strong R&B and funk influence. Here we are using a straight-sixteenths rhythmic subdivision, heard in a lot of contemporary jazz and R&B from the 1970s, onward.

The first 12-bar section features Dorian triads and 7–3 extended voicings in the right hand, over a root–5th or root–7th pattern, with rhythmic pickups in the left hand. The second 12-bar section features double 4th shapes, 7–3 extended voicings and blues scale phrases in the right hand, over a single-note pattern using more intense syncopation in the left hand. This blues progression is in A minor, based on example #7 from Chapter 4:

TRACK 64
piano only

TRACK 65
piano plus
rhythm section

Note the intense rhythmic interplay beween the hands, with the right hand using sixteenth note anticipations, and the left hand single-note figures frequently landing "in the spaces" between (or acting as pickups into) the right-hand voicings. These are all signature sounds in funk and R&B styles.

In the first 12-bar section, the right hand is playing Dorian triads on the Am7 and Dm7 chords: C, D and Em triads from the A Dorian mode, over the Am7 chord; and F, G, and Am triads from the D Dorian mode, over the Dm7 chord. Grace notes are used to connect into the 5th of each chord by half step. The dominant chords are voiced with 7–3 extended shapes (3–7–9 on the F7 and 3–7–#9 on the E7#9) alternating with upper structure triads (Dm built from the 13th of the F9 chord, and Fm built from the ♭9th of the E7#9 chord).

Meanwhile, the left hand is playing (and holding) the root of the chord on beat 1 of each measure, and is then playing either the 5th or the 7th of the chord in a staccato fashion during the measure, in a rhythmic conversation with the right-hand part.

In the second 12-bar section, the right hand is playing upper structure double 4th shapes, built from the 4th/11th, 5th, root, and 9th of the Am7 and Dm7 chords, and from the 7th of the E7#9 chord. The F9 chord is voiced using 7–3 extended (7–3–13), and in measures 21–22 some half-step "approaches" have been added to these dominant voicings. Drone-note phrases and fills are derived from the A blues scale in measures 14 and 24, and from the D blues scale in measure 18. Chromatically descending double 4ths provide some tension and color in measures 16 and 20.

Meanwhile, the left hand gets busier with more intense rhythms, still interweaving with the voicings in the right-hand part. Apart from playing the root on beat 1 of each measure, this single-note part is mostly landing on sixteenth note "upbeats," adding the 5th, 7th, and 4th/11th of the chord below the middle C area. On the E7#9 chord a root–3rd interval is used, to help define the dominant chord below the double 4th shapes in the right hand.

For more information on R&B/funk rhythms, comping and styles, please check out my companion volumes in this series, *R&B Keyboard* and *Smooth Jazz Piano* (both published by Hal Leonard Corporation).

Chapter 6
JAZZ-BLUES MELODIES AND SOLOING

In this chapter, we will see how melodies and solos are put together in jazz-blues styles. The pianist will normally play the melody or solo in the right hand, supported by chord voicings around the middle C area in the left hand. Often, these voicings will be either 7–3, 7–3 extended, double 4ths, or four-part upper structures. These shapes are sometimes referred to as "rootless" voicings when used in the left hand. When playing with a rhythm section, the root of the overall chord would typically be provided by the bass player. (In older styles some root–7th intervals in the lower register might also be played by the left hand.)

The play-along audio contains two tracks for each melody and solo example. The first track (which is at a slower tempo for the solo examples), has only the piano right-hand (i.e., the melody or solo part) on the right channel, and the piano left-hand voicings plus the rhythm section on the left channel. This enables you to practice the melody or solo using the right hand only, by turning down the right channel. The second track has the piano part (left and right hands) on the right channel, and the rhythm section on the left channel. This enables you to practice the melody or solo together with the left-hand voicings, by turning down the right channel. Of course, you're also encouraged to create your own melody and solo ideas over these progressions when jamming along with the band!

Generally, when distinguishing between melodies and solos, we could say that a melody is a predetermined sequence of notes, whereas a solo is an improvised sequence of notes. Keep in mind, however, that there is something of a "blurred line" between melody and solo playing in jazz-blues styles. As we have seen, most jazz-blues tunes use a 12-measure or 24-measure form, and this is the harmonic framework over which the melodies and/or solos will generally be placed. The source of most jazz-blues melodies and solos will be the blues scale. However, more advanced jazz-blues solos may incorporate additional scale sources, arpeggiated upper structures etc., as we will see later in this chapter.

Melodies using blues scales

Jazz-blues melodies (like the jazz-blues 12-bar form, as discussed in Chapter 4) can often be divided into four-measure phrases. In simple applications, the same 4-measure phrase might be repeated three times over the 12-measure blues form, otherwise the motif can be varied or developed. The most common melodic scale sources in jazz-blues are the blues scale built from the tonic (i.e., using a C blues scale over a blues progression in C), and the blues scale built from the relative minor (i.e., using an A blues scale over a blues progression in C). Note that some textbooks refer to these scale sources as "C minor blues" and "C major blues" scales, respectively (assuming the A blues scale is displaced to start on the note C).

Jazz-blues melodies, especially in the simpler styles, are often played "over the changes." This means that we are using notes within a scale related to the key (i.e., a C blues scale over a blues progression also in C), without particular regard for "landing" on certain notes as the chords change. In other words, we are not using a "target note" approach. This means that some vertical contradictions and/or dissonances may occur. This is not necessarily a problem, and indeed these tensions are a characteristic of blues styles in general. Also, the strong "linear," or melodic nature of the blues scale allows the ear to more easily forgive any notes which are "outside the chord."

Our first melody example uses notes from the C blues scale, over a basic blues progression in C:

Jazz-blues melody example #1

TRACK 66
piano RH on
right channel

TRACK 67
piano RH & LH
on right channel

The right-hand melody has various characteristics in common with many classic jazz-blues melodies, as follows:

- The 12-measure melody is constructed from a four-measure motif, repeated three times with some variations (this includes the rests at the end, which are an important part of the motif): In measure 3 we end with the descending phrase E♭–C, but in measure 7 this is varied using the ascending phrase B♭–C. In measure 11 we return to the E♭–C phrase (followed by some additional melody notes).

- Each four-measure motif starts later in the measure (on the "and" of 3 in measures 1, 5 and 9), and starts on an upbeat—all commonly used blues and jazz-blues rhythmic phrasings.

- Note the use of anticipations in the melody, particularly the anticipations of beat 1 in measures 2, 6, 10 and 12—again very typical.

The left hand is playing supportive 7–3 voicings (also using normal jazz-blues rhythms and syncopations) on all the dominant chords, just below the middle C area.

When you are comfortable playing the above melody, feel free to experiment with your own variations and melody ideas while playing along to the audio backing track!

The next melody example uses notes from the A blues scale, again over a basic blues progression in C (A being the relative minor of C):

Jazz-blues melody example #2

TRACK 68　　TRACK 69
piano RH on　piano RH & LH
right channel　on right channel

Note that this melody subjectively sounds more "inside" the chord changes than the previous melody—this is often the case when the melodic scale source is the blues scale built from the relative minor (A blues). For example, the third of the C7 chord (E, used in measures 4, 8 and 12), and the 3rd of the F7 chord (A, used in measures 2, 5 and 10), are good "target notes" or landing points on these chords, and these are available in the A blues scale but not in the C blues scale. (More about target notes later in this chapter.) Otherwise, a lot of the same rhythmic concepts (starting melodic phrases on upbeats, using anticipations etc.) that we saw in the previous example, are also being used here.

The left hand is playing 7–3 extended voicings on all the dominant chords: 3–7–9 on the C7 chord, and 7–3–13 on the F7 and G7 chords.

Our last melody example mixes together motifs from the C and A blues scales, over the same blue progression in C, as follows:

Jazz-blues melody example #3

TRACK 70
piano RH on
right channel

TRACK 71
piano RH & LH
on right channel

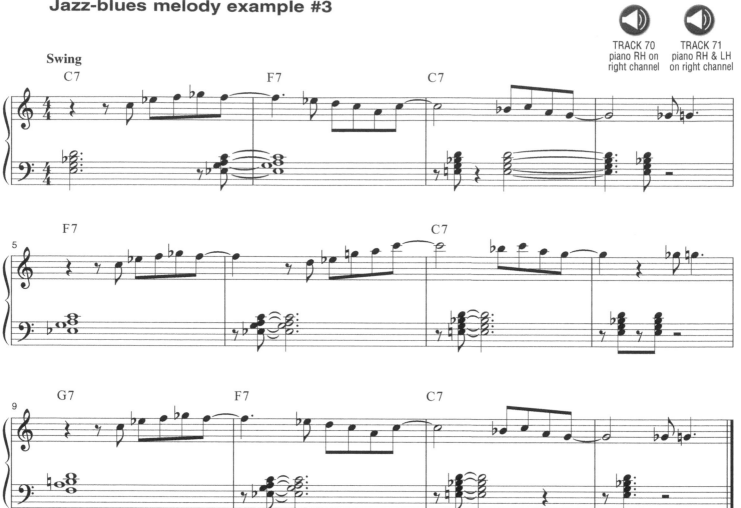

When combining notes from both the C blues and A blues scales as above, I would suggest not simply thinking of it as an expanded range of note choices available—these two scales together constitute three-quarters of all the available notes (C–D–E♭–E–F–G♭–G–A–B♭), which is not immediately helpful. Rather, it makes sense to think of "momentary restrictions" of notes, in other words, each motif can be derived from one scale or the other, in succession. Even if you quickly alternate between scales, this will still have the effect of shaping the melodic contour that results. The derivation of the above melody can be analyzed as follows:

- The phrase in measures 1, 5, and 9 (C–E♭–F–G♭–F) is derived from the C blues scale.

- The phrase in measures 2 and 10, starting on the "and" of 2 (E♭–D–C–A–C) is derived from the A blues scale.

- The phrase during beat 3 of measures 3, 7, and 11 (B♭–C) is derived from the C blues scale.

- The phrase during beat 4 of measures 3, 7, and 11 (A–G) is derived from the A blues scale.

- The phrase during beat 3 of measures 4, 8, and 12 (G♭–G) is derived from the C blues scale.

- The phrase in measure 6, starting on the "and" of 2 (D–E♭–G–A–C) is derived from the A blues scale.

At the points of chord change (frequently anticipated in the melody), basic chord tones are being used, for example the roots of both the C7 and F7 chords. Meanwhile, the left hand is playing four-part upper structures, building minor 7♭5th shapes from the thirds of all the dominant chords.

"Target note" and scale concepts

The concept of "target notes" was introduced when explaining the earlier melody example #2. A "target note" is a note within a chord which is a desirable "landing point" for a melody or solo, when played over the chord.

This is a common technique across the spectrum of jazz styles. More basic jazz-blues will not emphasize this technique, and will instead be more likely to use a blues scale over different chords (as previously noted for melody example #1). However, the greater the jazz influence becomes, the more likely we are to use the target note approach, to give us a framework around which a melody or solo can be developed. Normal target notes in jazz and jazz-blues styles are the 3rd, 5th, 7th or 9th of the chord. For altered dominant chords, the #5th and #9th are also useful options.

When connecting between target notes (as well as using the basic major, minor and/or blues scales related to the key signature), we might also use notes from different scales chosen on a chord-by-chord basis. On chord progressions which borrow from different keys (as in the II–V changes used in bebop blues), we can use different blues scales which relate to these "momentary" keys in the progression. There are also various scales available on altered dominant chords in jazz, including the melodic minor scale built from the ♭9th which is a jazz-blues favorite—more about this shortly.

Soloing with basic blues scales and phrases

With this in mind, we will now look at two jazz-blues solo examples. This first one is over a simple blues progression in G, and primarily uses the G blues scale (built from the tonic) and the E blues scale (built from the relative minor). Other common blues and jazz-blues techniques such as octave and drone-note phrases and crossover licks are also used. Although this more basic example is not conceived from a target note approach, note that the solo still "lands on" chord tones at the points of chord change much of the time.

Jazz-blues solo example #1

TRACK 72
piano RH on
right channel
—slow

TRACK 73
piano RH & LH
on right channel
—full speed

In the first chorus (measures 1–12), the right hand is mostly playing single-note phrases derived from blues scales, with some added grace notes. In measures 1–2, the solo phrase is derived from the G blues scale, leading into a phrase derived from the E blues scale from measure 3 (beat 2) until measure 4 (beat 3). During beat 4 of measure 4 we revert back to the G blues scale, and then we use the E blues scale for measures 5 and 6. We continue "alternating" between these two blues scales for the rest of the first chorus.

In the second chorus (measures 13–24), the right hand begins using octave figures for greater energy and impact, again alternating between the G and E blues scales. These are mixed in with "crossover" licks on the G7 chord in measures 15 and 19, similar to those derived earlier for tracks 56/57. Drone-note phrases from the G blues scale are also used in measures 16, 20, and 21, and from the G and E blues scales in measure 22. The 4th intervals in the last measure duplicate the top two notes of the 7–3 extended voicings in the left hand, one octave higher.

Meanwhile, the left hand is playing 7–3 extended voicings throughout this example: 7–3–13 on the G7 and A♭7 chords, 3–7–9 on the C7 chord, and 3–7–♯9 on the D7 chord. Again, we see that using 7–3 extended shapes can result in extensions and/or alterations being added. In this case the G7 and A♭7 are being upgraded to dominant 13th chords, and the D7 is being altered by adding the ♯9th (this is common practice on the V chord in jazz-blues styles).

Soloing with target notes, multiple scales and arpeggios

The second example is over a more sophisticated "bebop-style" jazz-blues progression in F, using various II–V chords and substitutions common to this style. Here we have a chance to apply more mainstream jazz soloing techniques, including target notes, alternate scales, and building arpeggios from upper structures available over the chords:

TRACK 74
piano RH
on right channel
–slow

TRACK 75
piano RH & LH
on right channel
–full speed

Jazz-blues solo example #2

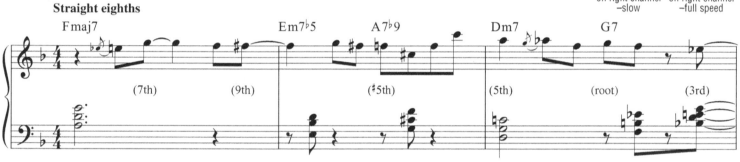

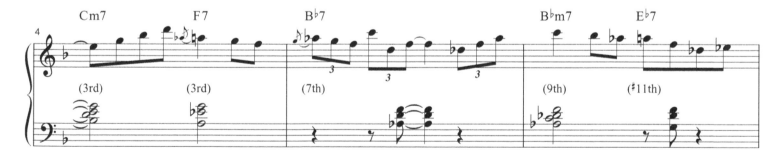

The target notes used on each chord are indicated between the staves, in brackets. The most typical ways to connect between the target notes in jazz-blues are to use the major scale built from the tonic (F major), the blues scale built from the tonic (F blues), or the blues scale built from the relative minor (D blues). All of these scales are used in the previous example, as well as some other scales and upper structure arpeggios which can be analyzed as follows:

- In measure 2 on the A7♭9 chord, all the notes are found within a melodic minor scale built from the ♭9th (B♭ melodic minor). This is a commonly used chord/scale relationship on dominant chords in jazz styles, as the scale contains all of the alterations: ♭5th, ♯5th, ♭9th and ♯9th. Also, the phrase over the A7♭9 can be thought of as a partial arpeggio of a four-part upper structure—a C♯maj7♭5 built from the 3rd of the chord.

- In measure 4 on the Cm7 chord, the solo uses an arpeggio of a four-part upper structure (an E♭maj7 built from the 3rd of the chord).

- Leading into measure 6 on the B♭m7 chord, the solo uses an arpeggio of a triad upper structure (a D♭ major triad built from the 3rd of the chord) during beat 4 of the previous measure, creating what might be called a "harmonic anticipation," outlining the new chord before the next downbeat.

- In measure 6, on the E♭7 chord, the solo uses an arpeggiated triad (D♭+) built from the 7th of the chord). This adds the 9th and ♯11th.

- In measure 7, on the Am7 and D7 chords, the solo phrase is derived from the A blues scale (built from the root, and 5th of these chords, respectively).

- In measure 13, on the Fmaj7 chord we are using a "crossover lick" similar to previous examples, but modified to end on the G minor triad built from the 3rd of the following Em7♭5 chord.

- In measure 16, on the Cm7 and F7 chords, the drone note phrase is derived from the C blues scale (built from the root and 5th of these chords, respectively).

- In measure 18, on the B♭m7 and E♭7 chords, the solo phrase is derived from the G blues scale (built from the 6th and 3rd of these chords, respectively).

- In measure 19, on the Am7 chord, the solo phrase is derived from the A blues scale (built from the root of the chord).

- In measures 21 and 24, on the Gm7 chord, the solo uses an arpeggio of a four-part upper structure (a B♭maj7 built from the 3rd of the chord).

- In measure 23, on the Fmaj7 and Dm7 chords, the solo phrase is derived from the A blues scale (built from the 3rd and 5th of these chords, respectively).

- In measure 25, on the C7 chord, the solo uses a descending arpeggio of a double 4th upper structure (7–♯9–♯5 on the C7 chord). This alters the chord by adding the ♯9th and ♯5th. These notes are also found within a D♭ melodic minor scale (built from the ♭9th of the C7 chord).

The left-hand voicings are a mixture of double 4ths, four-part chords, and 7–3 extended chords. Have fun playing the solos in this chapter, and then work on creating your own solo ideas by playing them along with the audio tracks. Don't forget to use the slower tempo versions at first, if necessary!

Chapter 7
STYLE FILE

In this chapter we have seven tunes written in different jazz-blues styles, and you'll get a chance to apply the techniques used by some of the most famous pianists in these styles. Each of these songs is based on one of the blues progressions outlined in Chapter 4, repeated for several choruses. Each chorus consists of 12 measures, except for "Hand Prints" which has a 24-bar structure, and "Canteloupe Rock" which extends the basic blues form to 16 bars by using a tag.

These tunes contain a mixture of comping or accompaniment, melody treatment, and improvised solo sections. However, in jazz-blues styles the lines between comping, melody, and solo are often blurred. For example, an accompaniment may still contain elaborate blues phrasings, and/or have a melodic component due to the voicings and top notes used.

These tunes were all recorded with a rhythm section as well as piano. On the audio tracks, the band is on the left channel, and the piano is on the right. To play along with the band, turn down the right channel. "Slow" as well as "Full Speed" tracks are also provided on the audio tracks for each song.

1. Duke's Blues

The first tune is in the jazz-blues swing style of Oscar Peterson. This is a mid-tempo, swing-eighths blues in C, based on progression example 3 in Chapter 4. In the first chorus (measures 1–12), both hands are playing the same rhythmic figures, creating polychords with different combinations of 7–3, 7–3 extended, triad and double 4th voicings. In the second chorus (measures 13–24), the piano solo begins in the right hand, supported by root–7th, 7–3, and 7–3 extended voicings in the left hand. The right-hand phrases using blues scales, ascending half steps, grace notes etc., are all signature jazz-blues techniques used by Oscar Peterson and others. In the third chorus (measures 25–36), the piano solo incorporates "crossover" and drone-note phrases. The fourth chorus (measures 37–49) is like the first, with fills in between the syncopated polychord voicings.

Make sure the rhythmic figures in the first and last choruses are cleanly articulated with both hands. Once you have the blues scales under your fingers, work on your own fills in the last chorus, and your own blues improvisation in the solo section!

TRACK 76
slow

TRACK 77
full speed

2. King of Cool

The next tune is in the "cool jazz" style of Wynton Kelly and Miles Davis. This is another mid-tempo, swing-eighths blues, this time in B♭ and based on progression example 1 in Chapter 4. Here the basic blues progression is varied by using the ♭VII chord (A♭7) in measures 11–12 of the form. In the first chorus (measures 1–12), the right hand is playing the melody using octaves and grace notes, often using the 3rd of the chord as a "target note." The left hand is supporting with root–7th or root–3rd–7th shapes, or 7–3 voicings used around the middle C area. In the second chorus (measures 13–24), the piano solo begins in the right hand, supported by root–7th, root-3rd, 7–3, and 7–3 extended voicings in the left hand. The solo at this point uses a combination of blues scale phrases (from the B♭ and G blues scales) and target notes, i.e., landing on the 3rds and 7ths of the dominant chords. Other devices such as drone-note phrases (measure 21) and upper structure arpeggios (measure 22) are also used. In the third chorus (measures 25–36), the piano solo continues, now adding octave phrases and more grace notes. In the fourth chorus (measures 37–48), the melody is re-stated, now with some "filled-in octaves," i.e., placing the 7th in between the 3rds in the right hand, as in measure 37 beat 1. Finally, we have a coda or ending section (measures 49–53), alternating between the I and IV chords (B♭7 and E♭7), using similar voicings to the last chorus.

Work on cleanly articulating the octaves and grace notes in the right hand (in the first and last choruses), and practice using the slower tempo first, if needed. When playing the solo section, note the upbeats used in some of the left-hand voicings, which create a rhythmic "conversation" with the right hand part. As you begin to improvise your own solo ideas, feel free to experiment with these rhythms "between the hands!"

TRACK 78
slow

TRACK 79
full speed

3. Hand Prints

Next up we have a jazz-blues waltz in the style of Wayne Shorter, featuring the polychord and double 4th voicings pioneered by pianist Bill Evans. This is in the key of C minor and has a 24-measure form (based on progression example 8 in Chapter 4). Here the minor blues progression is varied by using two different II–V progressions in measures 17–20 of the form. In the first chorus (measures 1–24), polychord voicings are created by combining double 4th shapes in both hands. This adds upper extensions (i.e., the 11th on both the Cm7 and Fm7 chords) to create a modern, transparent sound. The voicings also move up and then back down again in "parallel" half steps (in measures 2, 6, 10, 14 and 22), another common jazz technique. In measures 17–20 the right-hand motifs are derived from melodic minor scales, built from the 3rds of the minor 7♭5th chords and from the ♭9ths of the dominant 7(♯5♯9) chords. These are supported in the left hand by root–5th–7th and 7–3 extended voicings around the middle C area. In the second chorus (measures 25–48) the polychord voicings are interspersed with fills and drone note phrases from the C blues scale. The fills develop into a continuous solo over the II–V progressions in measures 41–44, using the same scale sources as explained above (for measures 17–20). The last eight measures of the form are then repeated (with the solo continuing) for a tag ending, in measures 49-61.

Make sure the polychord voicings and parallel half-step movements are articulated cleanly and evenly, and that the right-hand fills project over the left-hand voicings when they occur (for example, in measures 17–20). When you're confident enough, go ahead and add your own fills and solo ideas!

TRACK 80
slow

TRACK 81
full speed

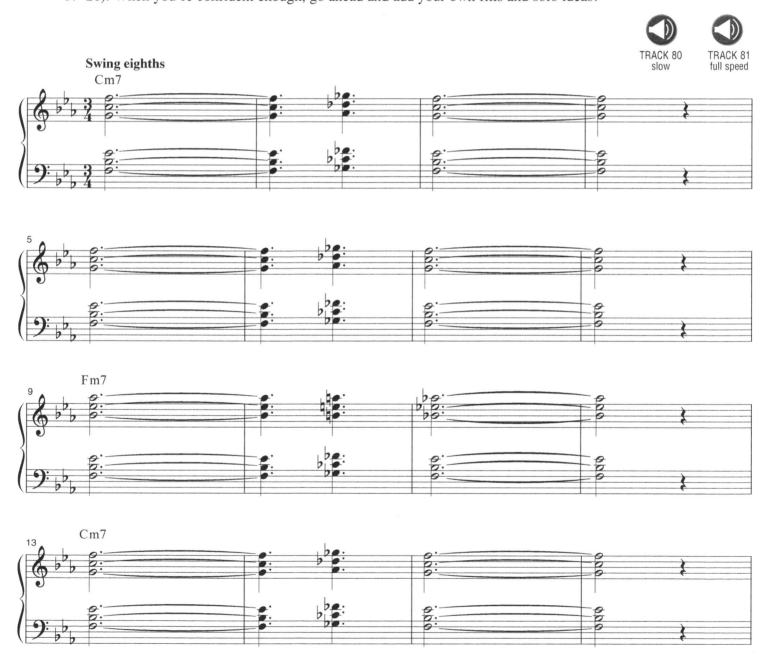

4. Soul Vacation

The next tune is in the "soul jazz" style of Mose Allison. This is a mid-tempo, swing-eighths blues in C, based on progression example 1 in Chapter 4, but with some substitutions and passing chords added. Here the first four measures of each 12-measure blues chorus is varied by alternating between the I and the V chords, creating additional momentum toward the IV chord in measure 5. The IV chord also moves up and then back down again by half-steps in measures 5 and 41.

In the first chorus (measures 1–12), the right hand uses a mixture of upper structure and Mixolydian triads, 7–3 extended voicings, and blues scale phrases with drone notes. The left hand is supporting with the root or with root–7th voicings. In the second chorus (measures 13–24), the right-hand part becomes more solo-oriented, adding grace notes and more drone note phrases, and scale-source runs (i.e., the E♭ melodic minor scale built from the 5th of the A♭7 chord in measure 21). In this chorus, some 7–3 and 7–3 extended voicings are also added in the left hand. In the third chorus (measures 25–36), the piano solo becomes more elaborate with busier blues scale runs, leading to the 3rd of the C7 chord in measure 35 as a target note, followed by a phrase derived from C Mixolydian. In the fourth chorus (measures 37–49), we return to the feel of the first chorus, now adding some chromatically descending 6th interval fills alongside the Mixolydian triads.

Make sure you observe the rests and articulate the staccato voicings cleanly in the first four measures of each blues chorus. Also, try to play the Mixolydian triad phrases as legato (smooth and connected) as you can, as this is important to the style.

TRACK 82
slow

TRACK 83
full speed

5. Blue Bop

Next we have a swing-eighths bop blues in the style of jazz piano icon Thelonious Monk. This is in the key of B♭ and is based on progression example 4 in Chapter 4, with some added passing chords and substitutions. Note the melodic motifs moving down by half steps, i.e., the A♭–G–G♭–F which connects from the 7th down to the 5th of the B♭7 chord in measure 1, and from the ♯9th down to the root of the F7♯9 chord in measure 9, etc. This is typical of Monk's phrasing style.

In the first chorus (measures 1–12), the right-hand melody often uses target notes such as the 3rd and/or 7th on the dominant chords, connected by blues scale phrases and chromatic half steps. These are supported by a mix of root, root–3rd, root–5th, root–7th, and root–10th voicings in the left hand. In the second chorus (measures 13–24), the piano solo begins in the right hand, mostly supported by syncopated root–7th voicings in the left hand (another signature Monk device). The solo at this point uses a combination of target notes, blues scale phrases, and some arpeggiated double 4th and 7–3 extended shapes. In the third chorus (measures 25–36), the piano solo continues, now adding more drone-note phrases and grace notes. In the fourth chorus (measures 37–48), the melody is re-stated, with some different fills in between the melodic motifs.

Monk had a rather "stark" playing style, and you can develop this sound by emphasizing the upbeats (i.e., on the left hand root–7th voicings during the solo) and by observing the rests. As usual, feel free to come up with your own fills and solo ideas once you are comfortable with the piece as a whole.

TRACK 84
slow

TRACK 85
full speed

6. Gospel Rider

The next tune is in the "soul jazz" style of Gene Harris, using his characteristic blend of blues, jazz, and gospel techniques. This mid-tempo, swing-eighths example is in B♭, and features a four measure intro leading into the first 12-measure blues chorus (which begins in measure 5). The chord progression used for the intro (in particular the ascending sequence in measure 3) is typical of various blues styles.

This tune uses a lot of Mixolydian triads in the right hand, which helps to impart the Gospel flavor. The intro uses Mixolydian triads in measures 1–2, as well as some triad, four-part and 7–3 extended voicings in measures 3-4, supported by a steady, eighth-note octave pattern in the left hand (another signature Gospel device). The intro progression and voicings are also used for the last four measures of the first and last 12-measure blues choruses (i.e., measures 13–16 and 49–52), and this section is repeated twice more to create a "tag" ending in measures 53–60.

In the first eight measures of the first chorus (measures 5–12), the Mixolydian triads are supported by more syncopated root–7th voicings and single-note phrases. The second chorus (measures 17–28) is busier and more elaborate, with syncopated polychord voicings, blues scale and drone-note phrases, Mixolydian 3rd intervals and crossover licks in the right hand, supported by 7–3 extended voicings in the left hand. The third chorus (measures 29–40) continues with octave phrases derived from the G and E blues scales, as well as drone note phrases and grace notes. The first eight measures of the fourth chorus (measures 41–48) restate the Mixolydian triad figure used in the first chorus, now an octave higher allowing the left hand to support with 7–3 extended voicings around the middle C area. Then the intro-feel returns in measure 49, leading into the tag ending as described above.

Make sure the octave patterns in the left hand are very steady and even, and that they rhythmically "lock up" with the right-hand shapes. Also, the "octave grace notes" in the third chorus (measures 29 and 33) require the thumb and 5th finger to simultaneously slide off a black key onto a white key. This can be tricky for the novice pianist, so feel free to omit these grace notes when first practicing the tune, if desired.

TRACK 86
slow

TRACK 87
full speed

7. Canteloupe Rock

Our last tune is in the "jazz rock" style of Herbie Hancock, and features the straight-eighths feel introduced by the fusion styles of the 60s and 70s. This piece uses progression example 6 in Chapter 4, adding a four-measure "tag" to the basic blues progression, creating a 16-measure form, in total. The comping figure in the first chorus (measures 1–16) uses thirds from Mixolydian modes in the right hand, with the root of the chord on top as a drone note. For example, in measure 1–4 the F above middle C is used as a drone note, above the third intervals C–Eb, Bb–D, A–C etc., from the F Mixolydian mode. Note that this causes "interior triad" movements to occur, i.e., we move between Bb and F major triads in the right hand over the F7 chord. The descending right-hand fill in measure 14 uses triads from the Bb Mixolydian mode over the Bb7 chord. Elsewhere, in the first chorus, the left hand plays the root of each chord every two measures, or at the point of chord change, and then the 7th, 6th, and 5th of each chord to double the top note of the Mixolydian third in the right hand, one octave lower.

In the second chorus (measures 17–32), the piano solo occurs in the right hand, supported by root–5th–7th shapes, triads, and 7–3 extended voicings in the left hand. The solo uses a combination of target notes, drone-note phrases from the F and D blues scales, Mixolydian third intervals, octaves, and grace notes.

In the third chorus (measures 33–48), we return to the comping groove used in the first chorus, now with various fills usings blues scales, drones, crossover licks, and Mixolydian triads.

In the first and last choruses, ensure that you hold the root notes played by the left-hand 5th finger for their full duration, as they need to be heard below the moving lines being played above. Also, some of the hand position changes in the last chorus (to play the fills added between the comping phrases) may be challenging. Try to "look ahead" as much as possible, and practice using the slow tempo track as needed. Have fun!

TRACK 88
slow

TRACK 89
full speed